The Financial Insider's Annuity Guide

FIRST AMERICAN PRESS

The Financial Insider's Annuity Guide

Copyright © 2010 by James Matthew Edwards

First American Press

ISBN: 978-0-9843763-0-8

Library of Congress Control Number: 2009943409

Printed in the United States of America

The Financial Insider's Annuity Guide

UNDERSTANDING ANNU
AND YOUR FINANCIAL POR

JAMES MATTHEW EDWA

Contents

Preface

During the financial crisis of 2008/2009, I received many phone calls and e-mails from individuals who were looking for annuity information. The information available over the internet was limited or did not pertain to the individual's particular situation.

I decided to surf the internet to see for myself exactly what annuity information was available. Unfortunately, what I found was limited in scope, and did not provide enough information for someone to make an informed decision. In some cases, the information was correct, but didn't explain why.

I was surprised by how many investment firms were writing about annuities but were limited to variable annuities with a very limited line of products to offer. There were also insurance companies who were writing about their specific products, but not about the full spectrum of information needed for a prospective client to properly evaluate.

It is my hope that this book provides you with a good barometer to help you weather any financial storm. I realize this is a lot of information, but I'm certain it will be beneficial for you, your family, and your financial portfolio.

This book represents 25 years of my professional experience and I am happy to share this information with you. I would be even happier if it provides you with the road map that leads to your financial success. I am sure once you evaluate all the information, you will find the information is worth more than its weight in gold.

Introduction

This book is designed to provide you with an understanding of annuities that only an annuity professional can provide.

Whether your goal is to maximize your return, provide safety of your principal, or to maximize your income for your retirement years, no other product available can accomplish so many financial goals as annuities. This book was written with you in mind and will help you accomplish your goals.

There are several reasons why you may have purchased this book:

Looking for Information – You have no idea what to do with your financial portfolio. What you have accomplished up to this point is no longer working. Your needs may have changed and you are looking for ideas and options for your financial portfolio.

Reducing Taxes – You are receiving Social Security and paying taxes on 50% to 85% of your Social Security income. You are looking for ways to reduce or to mitigate taxation as much as possible.

Lack of Diversification – You are realizing that all of your eggs are in one basket. You would like to re-balance your portfolio to maximize your return without any market risk, and you've heard annuities could be a good value added proposition.

Market Fears – You have lost so much that you're afraid to move your funds out of the market for fear of missing out on the market recovery. You're afraid to lose any more money since this is your entire life's savings. Maybe you're wondering how long will it take, if ever, to recover from your current market losses.

If you are an individual who thinks the best annuity products and rates are available at your local bank or a nationally recognized P&C company (Property & Casualty: A company that provides coverage for your auto and homeowner's policy), this book will change your mind. They offer what we call a rate of convenience, which I will describe briefly and more in depth later in this book.

Choosing a bank or P&C company is one of the biggest mistakes you can make that can cost you tens of thousands of dollars over the term of your annuity contract. Local banks and P&C companies know they will receive a certain amount of walk-in business.

They know that a certain percentage of those clients will purchase an annuity regardless of the current rates being offered, since they have banked with, or have been insured by these same companies for years. They know they don't have to offer the best rates available or be the most competitive in the market. They know consumers will purchase annuities from them because of their name recognition, trust, and the fact that they have already established a business relationship with them. They offer a rate of pure convenience; hence the term I like to use: "rate of convenience".

Many individuals accept the products and services offered through their banks and P&C agencies without ever considering or evaluating what other products the annuity market has to offer. It would be the same as buying a new car without ever seeing it, feeling it, touching it, or taking it out for a test drive. This is not an overstatement. Individuals will spend more time purchasing a new or used car than they will spend planning for their financial future. If this is you, read on and become enlightened!

Yes, I have a checking and savings account at my local bank and auto and homeowners policies with my P&C agency.

Yes, I trust them and the services they provide to me. However, I would never utilize their services to manage my financial portfolio, nor would I purchase an annuity from them.

I wrote this book for individuals who are serious about their money, who want to maximize their return, and get the biggest bang for the buck in a well-balanced financial portfolio. Remember these words: *well-balanced financial portfolio.* You will hear them over and over again. Individuals who want to benefit from my knowledge and expertise can utilize this information to meet their financial goals and objectives to benefit themselves and their families.

You'll be surprised to find that annuities are not as difficult to understand as you may think. *The Financial Insider's Annuity Guide* will provide you with a wealth of information, immediately at your disposal. It will be easy for you to follow and will show you each and every step along the way to help you determine which annuity is right for you. Not all annuities are created equal. Each and every annuity product is designed to accomplish or achieve different goals, concepts, and strategies.

You may have heard about clients who are dissatisfied with an annuity that was sold to them by an unscrupulous insurance agent. Today, there are so many different types of annuities that an agent would have to be inexperienced or willfully go out of their way to sell an inappropriate product to a client. There is a saying, "Buyer Beware". You should know: Which type of annuity are you purchasing? Why this particular annuity? Does this annuity meet or possibly exceed your financial objectives?

I am going to be the little guy on your shoulder telling you every move you need to make to double, triple, and quadruple your money. If income is your #1 priority, I will show you the entire process to maximize your income and get the best income rates available. I will also show you how to avoid costly mistakes that can dramatically affect your income at retirement. I will show you how you can double your retirement income by planning properly today for your retirement tomorrow.

After completing this book, you will be on the inside track just like the professionals, and you will have the ability to increase your own financial portfolio through the use of annuities. You will be able to safely and securely understand which annuities to purchase to give you greater returns, increase your net worth, and to enhance your retirement income. You will also learn the common pitfalls that can cost you dearly through taxation of Social Security income by as much as 50% to 85% and how you can avoid them. You will also know the primary factors that give annuities their strengths. Through annuities, you will find safety, security, guarantees, flexibility, versatility, options, and alternatives that no other product available on the market today can offer to you. This is why they are beneficial for so many financial portfolios. You can accomplish this without any market risk!

Why Annuities?

There has never been a single product, concept, or strategy that has withstood the test of time better than annuities. You may be surprised to learn that annuities have been in existence and used in various forms for over two thousand years.

There are over 2,500 insurance companies offering over 1,000 annuity products. I would be willing to bet that you've never heard of 99.9% of the companies or the products they offer. Many of these companies have the highest financial ratings and specialize only in the life and annuity business.

These companies are the leaders in the industry and produce the largest volume of annuity business. They have designed some of the most innovative products, crediting methods, benefits, and features available through annuities. They have also set the standard for other annuity companies to follow.

In Roman times, the common language was Latin, and annuities were referred to as "Annua". An annuity dealer, also known as a financial speculator, would sell an annuity for a single payment. In exchange, the annuity dealer would provide annual stipends to the client. The annual stipend, which would be of greater value including principal and interest, is paid annually during the individual's lifetime or over a predetermined period of time.

Domitius Ulpianus was one of the first annuity dealers in Rome and he created the first life expectancy table. The table was used to determine the average life expectancy for the citizens of Rome. The annuity dealer could determine the annual stipend based upon the total number of years the client (also known as the annuitant) might live according to the life expectancy table and the total amount invested by the client. Even today, all insurance companies who sell life, annuity, disability, and long term care insurance still use life expectancy tables. Normally, each company has their own Actuaries, who have significantly modified and updated the life expectancy tables within the last 2,000 years.

The annuity dealer was betting that he could get a better rate of return based upon the life expectancy of the client. If the client died earlier than projected by the life expectancy table, the annuity dealer would make a very sizable return on his investment. If the client's life expectancy were normal, the annuity dealer would make a reasonable rate of return over the client's lifetime. Finally, if the client lived longer than the life expectancy table, the annuity dealer could go bankrupt and may not be able to meet his financial obligations.

You can see the importance of having a life expectancy table to provide the most accurate data possible.

Throughout the last millennium, kings, queens, and rulers of European countries used annuities to fund their war efforts. They would promise to provide an annual stipend to wealthy landowners whose contributions directly funded the war. Naturally, as a landowner, it was important to be on the right side of war; otherwise you could stand to lose your money, your land, and possibly your head!

During the Great Depression, insurance companies were perceived as being stable institutions. Many investors chose to purchase annuities for the safety of principal, reasonable rates of returns, and guarantees associated with them. The insurance companies could provide guaranteed income streams and had the financial reserves to ensure they could meet the financial obligations of the policy.

Even during the financial turmoil of 2008/2009, annuities yet again proved their worth, exceeding $200 billion in annual sales and representing a "flight to safety" from market losses.

It's easy to understand the importance of annuities to any financial portfolio. Remember, they are the only financial vehicles that have withstood the test of time when safety, security, and guarantees were most important.

Information Technology

Today, we have one of the most powerful tools immediately available at our fingertips - the "Internet". We can find out just about anything by typing in a few words and hitting the "Enter" key. It's that simple! Or is it?

Yes, there are thousands of pages of information about any particular subject, along with hundreds of advertisers providing the best products and services that money can buy. They will direct you where you should go, how you can get it, from whom you can get it, and so on, but how accurate is the information? Are you getting all the information or just enough information to pique your interest? If you're not getting all the information or only part of the information, is it hurting you or helping you?

Have you ever heard the saying: "Sometimes, people have just enough information to be dangerous"? When it comes to the internet and annuities, everyone claims to be an expert. There is so much more to know about annuities than what you can find over the internet. When annuities are used properly, they can provide the best in safety, security, and guarantees to complete your well-balanced financial portfolio. Here is that phrase again: *well-balanced financial portfolio.*

This glut of available information is the main reason Google was one of the most highly anticipated IPO's (Initial Public Offering) and the most profitable companies to hit Wall Street. What Amazon did for books, Google's search engines did for internet advertising, even if that advertising serves only to sell useless products.

Every day, I have individuals contacting me about annuities and how they can obtain more information about them. I decided to surf the internet to find any information available regarding annuities. I was really surprised to find the limited amount of information about annuities, who was writing this information, and how much information was incomplete! Annuities are one of the most underutilized products available. Most people do not understand them or the advantages annuities can offer to balance and enhance any existing financial portfolio. I am confident that once you understand the advantages, you will quickly join the hundreds of thousands of individuals who collectively purchased over $200 billion in annuities during the last 12 months alone.

The original principal is guaranteed, grows tax deferred, and provides safety to any financial portfolio. This does not include **variable annuities**, since they are classified as a security just like stocks, bonds and mutual funds. Variable annuities are offered through securities licensed registered representatives and do not offer the same safety, security, and guarantees as other annuity products. We will get into the specific differences later.

Foundation for Building a Strong Financial Future

Before we can begin to focus on annuities in detail, we must first build or create a strong financial portfolio, beginning with the basics. Have you ever noticed, every time the stock market goes down, financial professionals come out of the woodwork and talk about how important it is to make sure your financial portfolio is diversified? Have you also noticed that most financial professionals' idea of *diversification* only relate to stocks, bonds, and mutual funds? I strongly doubt any financial professional has told you how to properly diversify your financial portfolio.

Imagine that you are building your dream house… tall cathedral ceilings, two story built-in custom bookcases, beautifully hand-carved fireplace mantle, stainless steel appliances, marble counter tops in the kitchen, complete with cedar lined closets, big open rooms that flow from one end of your house to the other, with large picture windows overlooking the valley on one side and ocean views on the other. What a beautiful and spectacular house you have built! As you walk up to the house in its entire splendor, you open the solid mahogany doors and walk inside onto uneven dirt floors throughout your entire new house! How could this have happened? Who could have forgotten to install the floors? Oops, the builder forgot to construct the complete foundation, which the entire house will stand upon. I realize this was a long, drawn out description; however, I needed you to understand the importance of diversification. Without it, you might as well build your dream house without the floors and without the foundation.

So, what is "diversification"? How can it help my financial portfolio? How do I properly diversify to protect my financial future?

Diversification is the foundation that your entire financial portfolio will be built upon. If the foundation to your house is stable, your house may shake and rattle in the midst of an earthquake, but your house will withstand the tremors and remain standing, long after the tremors subside. Just like your house, your financial portfolio should be able to weather any financial storm. It will, as long as you have taken the basic steps through proper diversification.

As an example, I'm sure you personally know individuals who have lost between 35% to as much as 50% of their entire financial portfolio between September, 2008 and the first quarter of 2009. If you asked them whether or not they would be able to recover, some will tell you they expect to recover over a period of time. Others will tell you due to current economic conditions, they will most likely never recover. These are usually older individuals who understand it will take time. This is why it is so important to understand why properly diversifying can be healthy for your overall financial portfolio. The most important key phrase is in the first sentence: "lost between 35% to as much as 50% of their *entire financial portfolio*…" They did everything right based upon what the financial experts advised them to do. They fully diversified between stocks, bonds, and mutual funds; however, they still lost 50% of their entire financial portfolio. *(Note: If you lost 50% of your entire financial portfolio, you need to make 100% return on your investment just to break-even. That's only to get you back where you started).* Were they able to weather the storm? No! Was their financial portfolio properly diversified? No!

What is the likelihood that someone could recover after experiencing a 50% loss in the market? The real answer is: only with the passage of sufficient time. Yes, the market will most likely recover in time, but can you afford to keep your funds at risk, in hopes of a future recovery? How long will the recovery take? Could it take 5, 10, 15, 20 or possibly 30 years? What if you just turned 50 years old? Will you be able to recover from such a huge market loss? That's a good possibility. What if you just turned 60 years of age? Maybe, if there were a quick recovery. What if you just turned 70 years of age? Not likely. What if you are older than 80 years of age? Probably not!

This brings up a very disturbing trend. Today, we are experiencing older clients investing 100% of their funds in the market, which is subject to 100% of the market risk. I certainly understand why anyone would want to maximize their return, but not at the risk of losing it all. Again, I am not opposed to investing. I'm just opposed to investing 100% of your entire financial portfolio in the market. Many seniors supplement their retirement from the returns in their investment accounts. They use the funds to supplement their retirement income, pay for medication, and for the elder care they receive.

As an example: If you had $1,000,000 and received a 5% gain, it would be equivalent to $50,000 of annual income. If the market lost 50%; the $1,000,000 would be reduced to $500,000 with no income benefit for the year. If you needed the additional income every year, you would be forced to take a withdrawal from your remaining balance, further reducing the investment account to $450,000. You would need to make 122% the following year to recoup 100% of your market losses for a full recovery. That would only bring your account balance to the original account value prior to any losses.

All investments in the stock market are subject to market risk. There are varying degrees of risk, which range between: conservative, balanced, and aggressive, and all are inherent to market risk. If you are one of those unfortunate individuals who lost as much as 50% of their entire financial portfolio, you will need to make 100% return on your investment to recoup 100% of your losses.

As a rule of thumb, most individuals can afford to be more aggressive until age 50. Between the ages of 50 and 60, clients should invest in a balanced or growth and income type fund. Beyond age 60, be conservative to preserve your principal. The **Rule of 100** is a very common rule and a good rule to use to determine acceptable risk. This is how it works: Take your current age and subtract it from 100; the balance is the maximum percentage that should be subjected to market risk. As an example: If you are age 72; minus your age from 100; equals 28. This is the maximum percentage (28%) of your financial portfolio that should be subjected to market risk. The balance of 72% should never be subject to market risk. This is your safe money and when combined with investment vehicles such as annuities, savings, and CDs, which offer safety, security, and guarantees, becomes your **safe money solution.** I will explain more about a safe money solution later. This is the rule of thumb that works very well for most individuals.

Here is an example that will make it even easier: A client is 45 years of age and has received $100,000 from her grandmother's estate. She has no idea what would be an acceptable investment.

EXAMPLE:

Rule of 100	100	
Current Age	– 45	
Balance	55	
Amount to be invested	$55,000	Subject to market risk
Balance after investment	$45,000	Safe Money Solution

Let's use another example using an older client. A client is 65 years of age and he has $300,000 for retirement. He has no idea what to do in his retirement years, but would still like to have a portion of his money invested in the market.

EXAMPLE:

Rule of 100	100	
Current Age	– 65	
Balance	35	
Amount to be invested	$105,000	Subject to market risk
Balance after investment	$195,000	Safe Money Solution

In light of this information, we can see that it's not okay for anyone, at any age, to be invested in the market 100% and subject to 100% of the market risk. ***EVER*****!**

That's not proper diversification. Proper diversification includes all funds, not just funds subject to market risk. This includes CDs, Annuities, Savings Accounts, Retirement Accounts, Stocks, Bonds, Mutual Funds, IRAs, 401(k)s, etc.   Any and all money should be included.

Even if you are a seasoned investor, the following information is good to review. If nothing else, it will provide you with information, which could be beneficial to you and your financial portfolio. You may have heard some of this information before or maybe it will provide you with a fresh perspective and ideas that could be worth considering.

First, I believe everyone should have an **emergency fund**. It should be 100% accessible. These funds should preferably be in a savings account or interest bearing checking account. The amount to retain in these accounts should be equivalent to 100% of your living expenses for a minimum of three months, to a maximum of six months. You may use CDs from your local bank, as long as you understand that you will be required to pay taxes every year on the gains. Should you need to liquidate your CD; a surrender charge will also be assessed. Annuities can also be used if you choose the right annuity that will eliminate surrender charges under certain circumstances. The advantage of using annuities is your funds will grow tax deferred. Most annuities offer a 10% penalty-free withdrawal annually.   Annuities are considered a safe money solution and will enhance any financial portfolio. This is due to the safety, security, and guarantees associated with them.

Second, after creating your emergency fund, you should begin saving in safe money solutions. You can use *fixed annuities* or *fixed indexed annuities*. Fixed annuities will provide you with a good rate of return and fixed indexed annuities will allow you to maximize your return. By using both, you will be able to hedge against deflationary interest rate environment and/or hedge against inflationary market trends.

Finally, open an *investment account.* Begin investing and constantly evaluate your investment objectives for your financial portfolio. If you are under age 50, you can afford to be aggressive because you have time to recover against market losses. I would still recommend no more than 50% of your financial portfolio be subject to market risk. As you get beyond age 50, you should begin to decrease your market risk according to your level of comfort with current market conditions. This is referred to as your comfort zone level.

What are risk tolerance levels and asset allocation models? Normally, when you open an investment account, the advisor will provide you with a series of questions for you to answer. Based upon how you answer the questions, they will determine your risk tolerance levels and they will provide you with your asset allocation model. By setting up your investment account according to your asset allocation model, it will help you remain within an acceptable risk tolerance level. This is a great way to initially set up your investment account.

Most individuals go through the program one time to determine their initial risk tolerance and asset allocation model. As the market goes up and down, it can dramatically affect the original asset allocation model in your financial portfolio. This is why it is recommended to evaluate and monitor your financial portfolio for changes, at least, annually. However, I would recommend between every six to twelve months. At that time, you need to determine whether you should re-balance or re-allocate your financial portfolio to keep within your original asset allocation model. Also, as you get older and experience life changing situations, your risk tolerance and asset allocation model may no longer meet your investment objectives. You should re-evaluate your risk tolerance and asset allocation model often for changes in your investment philosophy.

Unfortunately, very few investors actively manage their accounts properly. To ensure your investment accounts are managed properly, you need to ensure your account is properly allocated. Every six to twelve months, you need to evaluate and/or re-allocate your account to maintain your original allocation. As an example, if you invested 40% in a Growth and Income Fund, an additional 30% in an International Fund, and another 30% in a Money Market Fund, within six to twelve months, your allocation will automatically change with fluctuating market conditions. Your Growth and Income Fund may now account for 60%

of your investment account, International Fund may now be 15%, and finally 25% accounting for your Money Market Fund. As you can see, your investment portfolio is not the same as when you first allocated your account. To stay within your risk tolerance, you need to re-allocate your investment account. Without re-allocating your investment portfolio, your account will become severely out of sync from your original risk tolerance, which can place your entire investment portfolio at greater risk that you anticipated. Remember, risk tolerance levels and asset allocation model assessments are very methodical; investments are not, they're emotional. It's difficult not to get emotional if your account is down by 30% within a two-month period. This is why it is important to find a good financial advisor who can work with you. I will get into the role of the financial advisor later.

I discussed risk tolerance levels and asset allocation models. Now I would like to briefly discuss your internal risk tolerance, which I call your comfort zone level. Your Comfort Zone is defined as the amount you could comfortably or completely lose in the worst-case scenario. If the thought of losing 50% of your entire financial portfolio, makes you feel nauseous with fear, you need to reduce the amount you have invested. Find the comfort zone level that is acceptable for you, your internal risk tolerance level, and for your financial portfolio.

Again, I want to make it clear, I am not opposed to investing in the market or having a portion of your financial portfolio subject to market risk. I believe most individuals are **_not_** properly diversified and most are too heavily invested in the market without fully understanding the repercussions or the risk involved. The question is, will your financial portfolio have time to recover from significant market losses in a decreasing market environment?

Since most individuals are living longer, the need for seniors to maximize their return in their later years is becoming a major concern. If you invest too aggressively, you take a greater risk of losing what you have spent a lifetime to save. I feel there are other products, which are better suited for seniors that provide **_no_** market risk and could easily enhance any financial portfolio. Today, there are so many products available that will allow you to maximize your return, without any market risk, preserve your original principal, and protect the assets that it has taken a lifetime to build.

Should seniors invest? Absolutely! But... and this is a very big *but*; when the financial advisor's recommendation is to have 100% of your funds invest in the market and subject to market risk, something's not right. This is a big red flag and the first indication there's a problem. In such a case, I would be interested to see the senior suitability questionnaire, the asset allocation model, and the risk tolerance level located in the senior client's investment account file maintained in the registered representative's office.

As you get older, the need to assess your investment

objectives, risk tolerance, and your faculties must all be considered and become more critical. Your investment objective should be evaluated more frequently to ensure there are no life changing circumstances that your investment advisor should be aware of. This is to help protect you as you get older, preserve your assets, and guard your estate. Also, if you've had the same advisor for many years, they are getting older too. Regular calls to your advisor are critical to ensure you both have the same objectives and your faculties. It also helps to ensure that you or your advisor are not suffering from the initial stages of Alzheimer's or Dementia, which could dramatically affect your investment goals and your financial portfolio. I recommend, as you get older, to have a family member involved with your investment decisions. Having a third party involved helps to keep everyone honest and ensures there is no confusion concerning your financial objectives. This is to protect you, your family, your financial portfolio and your advisors.

Do you remember the client I discussed earlier whom had $1,000,000 invested in the market? If the same client had simply purchased an annuity offering a 5% guaranteed rate of return, the client could have an annual withdrawal for approximately $50,000 per year. Amazingly, the client could have achieved the desired results with **_no_** market risk; **_no_** loss of principal, and the income would have been fully guaranteed!

Your Financial Adv&.$*\... Who?

Yes, you're reading it correctly. I intentionally scrambled the letters to illustrate the confusion surrounding this issue. Your Financial Adv&.$*\... should read *"Your Financial Advisor"*. Today, it is very confusing because everyone in the financial services industry calls himself or herself a financial advisor. What does being a financial advisor really mean?

Before we can answer the question, we need to understand what has transpired to blur the lines of distinction. It comes down to one word: **Deregulation**, which ultimately was followed by the complete global meltdown of the financial services industry in 2008.

President Bill Clinton signed the *"Gramm–Leach–Bliley Act"* on November 12, 1999. This act was also referred to as the Bank Deregulation Bill and was passed on bipartisan support in the Senate, by a vote of 90-8. Prior to this bill being enacted, banks were limited by the *"Glass–Steagall Act of 1933"*; it separated banks which provided basic lending procedures such as business loans, mortgages, and checking/savings accounts from other banking institutions, which offered investment alternatives considered riskier investment choices.

Prior to deregulation, life was simple. Banks did banking, insurance companies issued policies, and investment firms invested other people's money. There was a clear and defined line that no one could cross and each industry had their regulators to ensure everyone remained within their appropriate borders. To cross borders, you had to be registered and/or qualified in the industry, essentially creating another career field. Very few individuals would cross industries unless, as an example, you were an insurance professional who sold variable annuities and variable life, which required the agent to be securities licensed and registered with the NASD (National Association of Securities Dealers), now referred to as FINRA (Financial Industry Regulatory Authority).

The descriptions for each financial services industry listed below provide generalized information for a basic understanding of each of their roles prior to deregulation. This is not a complete list providing detailed information about all aspects and descriptions of products and services offered by banks, P&C agencies, and investment firms. This is only a small representation as it relates to the average consumer.

You will notice each industry is clearly defined based upon the above criteria used for the products provided and the services being offered.

Banks: They provided mortgage loans, commercial loans, CDs, savings and checking accounts. Known as: *Bankers, Account Executives, and Account Reps*

Insurance Companies: They provided life, annuity, disability, and long term care insurance. Many companies specialized in P&C products only, such as: homeowner's, auto, etc. Known as: *Insurance Agents, Insurance Brokers, Chartered Life Underwriters, Chartered Financial Consultants, Financial Planners, and Certified Financial Planners*

Investment Firms: They provided stocks, bonds, and mutual funds. There are many other investment vehicles. However, I am limiting our subject matter for the average investor. Known as: *Stock Brokers, Investment Brokers, Investment Advisors, and Registered Investment Advisors*

In general, I have identified the three main financial industry groups and their titles, positions, descriptions, products, and services each group offers. *How many of you have CPAs and Accountants who are now financial advisors and financial planners?* The individual who has filed your taxes for years is now, suddenly, a financial planner. He has the ability to manage your investment accounts, open an on-line bank account for you, provide CDs, and still file your taxes in a timely manner.

Did you ever stop to think:

"How can he/she manage my investment account, keep up with the thousands of tax law changes each year, and provide me with good financial planning for life, annuities, disability, and long term care effectively?"

Now, let's multiply your situation with your current CPA who may have an additional 100 other clients who also utilize his/her services. If you haven't considered how effective he/she is about managing your investment account, maybe you should. Welcome to deregulation.

As you analyze each industry, can you clearly distinguish the differences "before" compared to "after" deregulation? Because the changes were so slight and occurred over time, the average consumer would not have noticed any difference at all, even though there were major changes.

Banks - Began providing term life insurance on-line, a few selective fixed annuities, and investment advisors for their walk-in clientele.

Security Firms - Began offering on-line banking, variable insurance products and advanced investments options for qualified and/

or accredited investors.

Insurance Companies - Commenced offering on-line banking, created investment products and investment portfolios in partnership with financial institutions, and administering tax qualified retirement plans, such as 401K's.

The most significant changes occurred at the executive and corporate levels. As an example: all financial institutions realized the revenue potential of acquiring *assets under management*. Additional profits were generated from bundling mortgage loans together as an investment vehicle, similar to stocks, bonds, and mutual funds. The profitability was so great that it encouraged financial institutions to offer mortgages, through the use of acquisitions and mergers and/ or working with mortgage banking firms to bundle mortgages within a portfolio as investments. These investments were offered and sold to institutional investors. Insurance companies and financial firms offered default bonds for a minimum fee, without understanding the total risk involved.

If an investor sought protection against the bundled mortgage financial portfolio becoming insolvent, he/ she could purchase a default bond for pennies on the dollar to protect his/her investment. Instead of buying a default bond or policy for their $50,000 investment risk, they could purchase a bond or policy for the entire portfolio of $50,000,000. If the portfolio defaulted, the bond or policy holder would receive the full value of $50,000,000 for their financial portfolio loss, even though their loss was limited to $50,000. This created another investment opportunity for investors who realized the magnitude of the sub-prime mortgage market. Instead of an investor insuring for the amount at risk, they could insure the entire portfolio. Several investors made millions, a few made billions, and the sub-prime mortgage market began to crumble.

Financial institutions also used life and annuity products for arbitrage, meaning that they purchased life insurance policies, bundled them together as an investment, and used immediate annuities for the maximum payouts to fund the minimum premium for the life insurance policy. The underlying guarantees in the annuities would hedge against the future cost of the life insurance policies and protect against longer life expectancies. Many investors used this concept of arbitrage to transfer their wealth on a tax-free basis. This also created the sale of life insurance policies in the secondary market for individuals who no longer needed or wanted to continue paying for their insurance policy. As you can see, anything and everything that wasn't nailed down was being bundled and sold in an overzealous investment market.

This is a quick overview and a simplistic explanation about the impact of deregulation, how it affects us today and will affect us for our future. Perhaps this helps you understand how the financial services industry became co-mingled and how everyone is classified as a financial advisor. Just because everyone considers himself or herself a financial advisor doesn't mean it's so. I want to get one thing straight and I want it to be very clear…*there is no such thing as a financial advisor.* There is no professional designation or class you can take to be classified as a financial advisor. It is a generalized term that came about with deregulation and is used very loosely in the financial services industry.

The same holds true for financial planners. The term financial planner is very broad, but many financial planners specialize in certain areas of expertise. As an example, there are financial planners who specialize in saving for retirement, others who specialize in generating income for retirement, and financial planners who specialize in transferring your wealth to the people you love and care the most about in this world on a tax-favored and/or tax-free basis. They are all financial planners. However, very few can do all three effectively.

There are Certified Financial Planners, Registered Investment Advisors, Registered Representatives, Chartered Life Underwriters, Chartered Financial Consultants, and other registered and recognized designations, but there is no designation for a financial advisor. Let's use the titles, which correlate to the job descriptions, prior to deregulation. It makes it so much simpler and easy to understand!

Banks, Property & Casualty Agencies, and Annuities

L et's acknowledge what each financial industry did well prior to deregulation and are returning to now. Many have been forced through the turmoil of 2008 to go back to the basics, increase their capital reserves or choose to follow in the footsteps of their counterparts and fail. Many of the issues still plaguing the financial services industry are the result of capital reserve requirements. Credit rating firms use these limits to determine whether to increase, hold, or decrease credit ratings for each financial services firm. The ratings could result in either an increase in capital reserve requirements or a downgrade to the financial firms' credit rating, which could be detrimental and further increase the capital reserve requirements.

Remember, prior to deregulation, banks were limited by the *"Glass-Steagall Act of 1933"*, from engaging in risky investments.

Banks generally offered mortgages, CDs, checking, and savings account, etc. Would I purchase a CD from a bank? Absolutely, since banks specialize in CDs. I would utilize it as a safe money solution or as a percentage of my emergency fund. Similar to most individuals, I'm sure you have a local bank that you conduct business with, and normally, if you were in the market for a CD, you would more than likely purchase it from your local bank.

If I were in the market to purchase an annuity, would I purchase an annuity from my local bank? Absolutely not! There are many things that banks do well; annuities are not one of them. Banks are known for having high turnovers with their employees, so who you work with today may not be there tomorrow. They are limited to who can sell annuities in each branch, since they must have an insurance license to sell annuities. Also, having two or three annuities at your disposal in a local bank does not make you an expert or an annuity specialist. Typically, banks offer basic annuities with a fixed rate of return only. There is so much more to annuities than the limited training bank employees receive to properly educate them or make them an expert in annuities. Most bank employees do not understand the broad scope and variations available with annuity products. Remember, there are over 2,500 insurance companies and over 1,000 annuity products. An annuity specialist may not know all the annuity products available from each company, but certainly has the knowledge and expertise to explain any type of annuity available today. I have never known of any bank that was able to provide the most competitive products and rates available in the annuity market. Since the selection of annuities is very limited by banks, clients would only be purchasing a product, instead of incorporating the annuity as part of their financial portfolio designed to meet their needs, objectives, and goals for their financial future.

Again, banks offer basic fixed annuity products, which have limited capabilities. They typically have between two to three annuity products they can offer. These are the same products they have been selling for the last 30 years. They are not the most competitive products and the employees' knowledge about annuities is limited to only the few products they sell.

Unfortunately, the same holds true for P&C agencies. Just because a P&C agency sells insurance products, doesn't mean to say they offer the best life, annuity, disability, and long term care products available. Yes, there are P&C agencies that offer a complete line of insurance products such as annuities, but don't be fooled into thinking that your P&C agency can provide you with the best of everything in the insurance world. If this were true, there would be only one insurance company in North America and they would be filing for bankruptcy due to the high claims rate they have experienced in the last year alone. They want you to believe that they are the best so you will conduct business with them and be happy with your rate of convenience.

I know there are many of you out there who may be a little skeptical about the information I am writing about or you feel very confident about your bank and P&C agency's ability. So here is my challenge to you: The next time you stop into your local bank and P&C agency, ask any employee...

"What is a fixed indexed annuity?"; " What makes fixed indexed annuity so different from other annuity products?"; and, "What are the various crediting options available for an fixed indexed annuity?"

I would be very surprised if they could answer anything other than to say, "I don't know!" Again, their knowledge and expertise regarding annuities is limited to the products they have available in their local branch and P&C agencies, only!

The Financial Market, Your Financial Portfolio, and Annuities

Banks and P&C agencies offer products and services beyond the scope of annuities and the financial services industry. I have been conducting business with my local bank and P&C agency for many years and I trust them implicitly in their area of expertise. I understand what they do well and I also know their limitations. If interest rates decrease and I am considering re-financing my house to reduce my monthly mortgage payment, I would want to get the three best bids available from three completely different sources. The first would be from my local bank. Second, would be from an independent mortgage broker who works with several lending institutions. Finally, third, from a lending institution that is 100% on-line. The reasoning behind the bids is to keep everyone honest and ultimately get the best rates available.

Just because I do business with my local bank does not automatically entitle them to all my business. If they would like to keep my business, they should be as competitive as possible by offering me the best rates available. They have my financial information and know my spending habits, along with the history of my account balances. Some may say my actions show no loyalty to my banking institution. I feel this is a business driven relationship on a two way street. They certainly have the opportunity to earn my business since I have been conducting business with them for years. I'm more concerned about my family and our financial well-being than the bank. I'm not going to pay higher interest rates to have the privilege of conducting business with my bank without considering other options and alternatives from other financial institutions.

I take the same approach when it comes to my P&C agency. When I receive a rate increase, I question why I received the rate increase and ask what can be done to change, modify, or adapt my policy to reduce, or make up for, the increases.

Today, there is no loyalty between you and your local banks or your P&C agencies. The days of knowing the local banker who works and lives in the community and who has been there for over 30 years are gone. You can no longer conduct business based upon your word and a handshake. They have been replaced with lawsuits and judgments. If you think I'm wrong, call your local banker and tell him you're going to be a few months late paying your mortgage! Or call your P&C agency and tell them your sixteen year old daughter just had a major accident and both cars involved were totaled, but you can't afford a rate increase right now!

Of course, they are running a business and need to be as efficient, effective, and as profitable as possible. Have you ever heard the saying: "*The rich get richer and the poor get poorer*"? Perhaps there is a reason why this happens. Maybe it's because the rich manage their finances like a business, instead of simply accepting the increases without asking the question: Why? And what other alternatives are available to reduce their cost? Maybe the rich took the time to evaluate the cost versus the return for the money being spent. We should be asking ourselves: "*Is it possible to get the same service for less? If so, can I save the difference and use it for investing?*" Begin by managing your finances like a business and keep as much of your money in your own pocket, instead of someone else's pocket, such as banks and the P&C agencies.

I know a lot of good bankers who know how to take care of their clients. I know many individuals who own their own P&C agencies. I also know many individuals who are in the financial services industry as registered investment advisors and registered representatives for securities. There are many professionals in the financial services business who provide an incredible and valuable service for their clients. Unfortunately, many of them are limited to the resources available from their firms.

Recently, I had a conversation with a friend who is a Registered Investment Advisor. I asked him, *"Has the financial turmoil of 2008/2009 affected your business?"* He looked at me, smiled, and said, *"It's had no effect on my business, ZERO!"* He continued, *"My clients didn't make any money, but they didn't lose any money either. When the market started going crazy in September, October, November, and then hit an all time high of 14,000, I knew it was time to bail and protect my clients' assets. I called all my clients and told them I was going to move them to the safest money position I knew of…CASH! They were very happy since many of my clients' friends lost 35% on average from their financial portfolio."* He did everything he should have done; managed their assets, provided a good rate of return, and protected their assets against significant market losses.

All too often, the **investment advisor** focuses on providing a reasonable rate of return; which is only one aspect of managing an investment account. There is also another aspect that goes hand in hand with asset management, which is risk management! Too many times the risk factor is over-shadowed by market returns, without any consideration for protecting the gains against future market declines.

In this section, I will be describing the role of your investment advisor (*not to be confused with financial advisor; as I previously stated: There is no such thing as a financial advisor*). To keep everyone on the same page, let's define the investment advisor as someone who makes investment recommendation, manages your assets, and/or provides investment advice. Some of the information I am going to write about, you may or may not agree with. Whether you agree or disagree, this information is about you understanding your role and the role you play in managing your financial portfolio and the role of your investment advisor.

Let's get started. First, I want you to understand your investment advisor is not your friend, nor should he/she be your friend! Not only should he/she not be your friend, they should not be a family member either. It's very difficult to separate family, friends, and your personal relationships, with business. This is an internal conflict, which can only lead to a financial disaster. Yes, there are a small percentage of situations, which work out well. Everyone makes money, remain close family and friends, and can walk away at some future point in time, while maintaining the relationship. This is not the rule, but the exception to the rule. When everyone's making money, everyone's happy. But when you're losing money hand over fist and your financial future depends on the ability of your investment advisor, it's hard to retain the relationship with family and friends without getting emotional. As an example; there is a current court case where a well-known celebrity is suing his father and his uncle in the amount of $4,000,000. This includes the original loan amount of $870,000 dating back to 1984, to purchase an investment property in Los Angeles, California. The additional increase was derived from unpaid interest.

This is a perfect example of why you should treat your finances like a business. It is all too common for celebrities to find themselves in the midst of a financial scandal. Unfortunately, there are so many more stories you've never heard about, until they become a tragedy on the front page of every publication and on the homepage of every news agency website.

There's a saying: *"If you want to keep your family and friends forever, never loan them any money or go into business with them. If you do, money will get in between the relationship and you will risk losing your family and friends forever. If you don't, they may get angry for a time, it will pass, and you will keep them as family and friends, forever"*. Whoever said this must have been a very wise person!

There are also individuals who have become friends with their investment advisor after years of being a client. This is a big mistake. I'm not saying that you shouldn't be friendly. I'm saying that there should be a clear and distinct line between you and your investment advisor. It should resemble more of an employer/employee relationship. "Why?" you might ask? It's difficult to fire friends and terminate the relationship. Over the years, you have grown to like this person; he/she shares investment ideas and strategies with you and made recommendations, which you have profited from. You have spent hours and hours over the phone and in person, talking about the family, the job, the kids, vacations, and what you are going to do, once you retire. So how can you fire them? Have you no loyalty?

What about their kids? What will their family do if you fire them? How will they survive, knowing times are tough, even though they lost 35% of your financial portfolio? After all, the market average was down 35% across the board.

This isn't about your investment advisor; this is about you, your spouse, your family, your dreams, your retirement goals, and your adventures.

The investment advisor was hired by you to perform a very specific task. You are paying for his/her knowledge, experience, skills, and the ability to manage your assets, which includes risk! For assets under management, the investment advisor is being paid whether you increased or decreased your account value or if the market is up or if the market is down - it doesn't matter - he/she still gets paid. No one has a problem paying an asset fee when the market is up; but is sure does come into play when the market is down. Now you can understand why I say it should be more of an employer/employee relationship and you should hold your investment advisor accountable for managing both profits and risk.

So, how does your investment advisor rate? Maybe you currently do not have an investment advisor and want to know how to find a great one. If so, this is a great place to find out what to look for in an investment advisor and what qualities that make them great.

I love the old Spaghetti Westerns, so let's use the proverbial rating system of the old west: The Good, The Bad, and The Ugly - let's go over all three to see how your investment advisor rates. This is the point where you have to be honest with yourself; after all, it is your financial portfolio and your financial future!

The Good - This really should be the great! This is the investment advisor who may not give you the biggest return, but always provides you with a better than average return. If the market is up +18% for the average, your account was up +20%, +2 points better than the market average. He also manages your risk; meaning that when the market goes down -20% for the market average, he/she has already spoken to you, made adjustments to your portfolio and your account was down -10% for the year, instead of the market average.

The Bad - The bad is the average, meaning that whether the market is up or down; you always end up receiving the market average. As an example, in 2008, the market average was down 37%, so your account was down 38%, which is close enough to be classified in line with the market average. If the market averaged 18% up for the year, then your account was up 16% for the year. Again, it would be in line with the market average even though it wasn't exact.

I'm not writing about a fluke year or a few years

that equaled the market average, but an investment advisor who consistently follows the market average. Naturally, you have to evaluate the overall returns and determine whether you're happy with the investment advisor's return on your investment, before you make the determination to keep your investment advisor or make a change. As an example; mimicking the performance of the *S&P 500 Index* ® could provide you with a very lucrative return. However, if your account followed the market average and provided an average effective yield of 4% for the last 10 years, you may not have been happy with those returns and expected a greater return on your investment. Unless you're happy with your returns and with these results, there may be a few questions you need to ask yourself:

"If my investment advisor is providing me with the market average, what do I need him for? Maybe I need to find a new investment advisor who is great!"

The Ugly – This is the investment advisor who loses money when the market goes up, loses money when the market goes down, and loses money when the market goes sideways. This truly is someone who shouldn't be in the financial services industry, unless, of course, he/she is working with safe money solutions only, such as annuities, which are not subject to any market risk.

I have explained the role of the investment advisor. Now, I would like to explain the role of variable annuities, and their relationship with the investment advisor and the investment firm. Even though an investment firm is offering or advertising variable annuities with their particular name on it, the contract is underwritten and issued by insurance companies. This is known as a private label variable annuity contract. All annuities, whether it is a private label annuity, variable annuity or a fixed annuity contract, are all underwritten and issued by an insurance company.

Most investment advisors' objective is to acquire assets under management, since this is how they are compensated. They do not recommend the sale of annuities, except for variable annuity products, which fall in the category of assets under management. Regardless of the type of annuity (variable or fixed annuities), all annuities are insurance products, and you must be insurance licensed to sell them. The investment advisor's broker-dealer must also approve any and all annuity products and annuity companies sold by their investment advisors.

If an investment advisor is not insurance licensed, he/she cannot sell variable or fixed annuity products. When they are not properly licensed, most advisors will recommend to their clients **_NOT_** to purchase annuities, giving no other explanation than they can receive a better rate of return by investing directly in the market, than investing in a variable or fixed annuity contract. Again, whether an investment advisor is insurance licensed or not, they get paid for acquiring assets under management and variable annuities are included in the assets under management fee; fixed and fixed indexed annuities are excluded.

Even though I am not a big fan of variable annuities, there are features that I do like such as the M&E (Mortality and Expense) charges that allow for the death benefit within the variable annuity contract, and the income benefit rider, which provides a client with a guaranteed income stream, regardless of market performance. Keep in mind that the benefits of the income benefit rider have been reduced since the meltdown of 2008 and the fees associated with them have increased. Make sure you read all of the disclosures before you purchase a variable annuity contract and the provisions of the riders.

Even though a securities registered representative may be insurance licensed, it doesn't mean to say that they understand fixed annuities, how they work, or the different type of crediting methods, and so on.

This is not about investments vs. annuities, or registered representatives vs. insurance agents. This is about you understanding each of their roles and how it pertains to you and your financial portfolio. It is important to take control and understand how to properly diversify to have a well-balanced financial portfolio. You should understand how each of the products work together as an integral part of your financial portfolio to compliment each other. Every role within your financial portfolio plays a vital part in helping you secure your financial future. Your financial portfolio should be similar to an orchestra with many different instruments playing different parts in the musical arrangement, creating beautiful music in harmony, which is soothing to your ears... and to your financial future. You must take complete control and responsibility of your financial future and hold others accountable for their actions to achieve your desired results for your financial goals.

The Dream Team

Throughout the world, Europeans are known for being the biggest, craziest, and most uncontrollable soccer fans in the world (In Europe, they call it football, in America, we call it soccer). Similarly, Americans are known for being avid basketball fans. Americans love their favorite basketball teams and their favorite players. We show our loyalty to our teams and our players by wearing their jerseys on our backs, painting their colors on our face, and supporting them whether they win or lose.

In 1989, the FIBA; which is the French acronym for "Federation of International Basketball Amateur" of the Olympics Games was changed, dropping the term "Amateur", which now allows professional basketball players to compete in the Summer Olympic Games. It is still FIBA, since the first two letters in Basketball (BA) still complete the French acronym: "Federation of International Basketball".

In 1992, the world of basketball changed forever!

For the first time ever, a team consisting of the best professional basketball players that America had to offer came together to play as one team ("The Dream Team" from the USA) at the Summer Olympics Games. There was not a country, a team, or a player, who would not have wanted to play against "The Dream Team". Even if they lost, they would have been in awe just to say they played with the greatest players, the best of the best, and the legends of the sport that made basketball what it is today. Can you image the impact of having the best players in the world, under one roof, and playing on the same team for America? Unbelievable! That's the team you've always dreamt about, "The Dream Team". Need I say more?

The 1992 Summer Olympics held in Barcelona, Spain hosted the first professional Men's Basketball Team competition. "The Dream Team" won their first gold medal in the Olympics utilizing professional basketball players. The USA received several gold medals during the Olympics following the 1992 Summer Games. Unfortunately, everything came to an end in the Summer Olympic Games of 2004. Argentina received the gold medal, Italy received the silver medal, and the USA's "Dream Team" received a bronze medal.

Even though the USA had the best professional players for the 2004 Olympics Games, it is still a "team" sport, not an "individual" sport. Because the 2004 team played in the All-Stars Games in the USA prior to the Olympics, it never allowed much practice time for the Olympic team. It takes the entire team, working together, to bring home the gold.

There are many memorable team moments such as: the US hockey team, "The Miracle on Ice", beat Finland 4-2 to win the gold medal for the Winter Olympic Games in 1980; or the Boston Red Sox who won the World Series against the St. Louis Cardinals in 2004. That was the first time that the Boston Red Sox won the World Series since 1918, breaking the "Curse of the Bambino" for trading Babe Ruth in 1919 to the New York Yankees. Michael Phelps, who received 6 gold medals in 2004 in Athens, Greece and 8 gold medals in Beijing, China during the Olympic Games in 2008, has won more gold medals in a single Olympic Game and the most gold medals than any other Olympian in history. However, it still required the best swimmers as a team to win the 4 X 400 meter freestyle relay, the 4 X 200 meter freestyle relay, and the 4 X 100 meter medley relay for him to accomplish this feat.

It's the same with your financial portfolio; it is also about the "team", not a single individual. If you want to bring home the gold for your financial portfolio, you must create a professional team working together to develop and manage your assets as a well-balanced financial portfolio.

All too often, I hear about professionals who are discussing new concepts and strategies with prospective clients, only to have the clients respond with, "*I would like to discuss this matter further with my trusted financial advisor to see how this concept and strategy may be implemented into my financial portfolio."* Today, we now know when someone uses the term financial advisor, they are using the term very broadly or are unaware of their advisor's true title or professional job description. Depending on the concept, strategy, and the ability of your advisor, they may not have the experience or expertise to provide you with the best financial advice. Under normal circumstances, the advisor does not want to give the impression he/she does not understand, thus diverting the attention to products he/she does understand and can comfortably discuss. As an example, let's say someone spoke with you about a safe money solution using fixed annuities or fixed indexed annuities (you will be able to understand the differences between the two shortly). Then, you speak with your investment advisor and he/she recommends a variable annuity (which is subject to market risk and not classified as a safe money solution), or recommends adding bonds to your financial portfolio. Bonds, which typically decrease in value in an inflationary market, must be held to maturity to avoid possible market risk. They are not the same as a true safe money solution which uses fixed annuities and/or fixed indexed annuities, and do not provide the same safety, security, and guarantees, without any market risk.

I'm sure you've heard the classic rhyme, "The Butcher, the Baker, and the Candle Stick Maker". What if, instead of three individuals specializing in three completely different professions, you had one specialist working in all three professions? What do you think the probability of something going wrong would be? Unfortunately, this is the situation most individuals find themselves in today, using one advisor who manages their entire financial portfolio.

Previously, I provided you with a good realization: *"This isn't about your investment advisor; this is about you, your spouse, your family, your dreams, your retirement goals, your adventures."* Ultimately, the responsibility of your financial portfolio is yours and yours alone. Even if you choose to have someone manage your account, you still need to hold the advisor accountable to provide a reasonable rate of return in reference to your expectations for your financial portfolio.

Who should your financial "Dream Team" consist of professionally? Simplistically, it should consist of three professionals: an investment advisor, a financial planner, and an account representative.

> *Investment Advisor* – The individual who manages your investment assets and risks would be classified as your investment advisor.

> *Financial Planner* – This is typically an insurance broker who specializes in annuities and can provide you with safe money solutions.

> *Account Representative* – The individual from your local bank who provides CDs, emergency fund, and other products and services to benefit your financial portfolio.

This is a representation of the growth stage of your financial portfolio in its entirety. All three elements need to work in unison with each other, not in conflict with or in opposition to each other.

Please keep in mind that the initial financial dream team is going to change as your financial situation changes. In the beginning, the role of your account representative at your local bank will be working with you to help you create an emergency fund in case of emergencies in the future. Once it is set up and funded, it should only require an annual review to make sure it still meets your needs and objectives. The role of the account representative will decrease over time, except for the annual review, which must be an annual requirement.

The financial planner will initially set up a life and disability policy to protect you and your family against premature death and from you becoming disabled. This is to ensure that you and your family are protected and your funds are available when you need your funds most. This is normally the period in your life when you're making the least amount of money. Since these policies cost virtually pennies on the dollars, the money spent is worth the protection and peace of mind of knowing that you and your family are protected. Again, the financial planner will provide an annual review to make sure there are no major changes in your life. The role of the financial planner will also decrease after your needs have been met. The role of the investment advisor will increase as your funds are being invested and allocated for growth. This is going to change again as your investment account grows and you get older. You will need to diversify into a safe money solution and your financial portfolio will also need to be re-allocated to a conservative and well-balanced financial portfolio. Eventually, retirement income will become a major focus, along with the need to preserve and protect your entire financial portfolio. The roles of your advisors will change again as your financial portfolio changes to a conservative portfolio and the role of the financial planner becomes more prevalent. This is to ensure you have the income to sustain you and your family for a lifetime and create a legacy for your family to remember.

The investment advisors role will initially be minimal, once the emergency fund and the life and disability policies have been set-up and established to protect you and your family. As your income grows, and you have more disposable income to invest, the need to work with your investment advisor becomes more critical. After you have invested and built up your account, you may want to discuss ways to preserve a percentage of your financial portfolio, using the Rule of 100 with both your investment advisor and your financial planner. Both, and sometimes all three professionals, may need to work together for the common good, and what is in the best interest for you and your family. If your advisors cannot work together, find ones who can. This isn't about their egos. It's about you, your family and your financial portfolio.

I made my choice a few years ago to provide concepts and strategies using only safe money solutions. There were two reasons, which lead to my decision: First, the market has been extremely volatile since 2000. Second, the products being designed today allow clients to maximize their return, without any market risk. I no longer have to worry if a client will lose 50% of their financial portfolio overnight. It is impossible to lose money using safe money solutions with fixed annuities and fixed indexed annuities. Absolutely none of my clients have lost money in annuities as a safe money solution. I have spoken to literally thousands of individuals, who would much rather receive a zero rate of return (without loss of principal), instead of the -37% loss they received in September, 2008 from their financial portfolio.

I know many of you will say it's only a paper loss... or maybe that's what your investment advisor has told you? Isn't it funny that it's only the investment advisor who will tell you: "*It's only a paper loss if you sell?*" At some point in time, the market will have to come back or you will want to sell your positions in order to qualify for the deductions on your tax return. I will never understand why individuals would want to fool themselves or place their head in the sand when it comes to their financial portfolio: "*My portfolio is down 50%, but it's only a paper loss; I don't actually lose the money until I sell, so I still have 100% of my financial portfolio!*"

Why do we do this to ourselves? Why do we accept

it? That's like saying, "*My house is on fire, but let's see how much of it burns before I call 911! Maybe it will only burn a little!*" The moment my house caught on fire, I would be dialing 911 asking them to send a fire truck as soon as possible. I would be grabbing a fire extinguisher and trying to contain the fire as much as possible, before the fire trucks arrived. Similar to the house catching on fire, if your investment account is down 50% and you do nothing, what is the probability your account will come back?

I have a client in his 70's named Bob who's a retired hedge fund manager. His net worth is in excess of $14 million, but he has grown tired of investing and trading every day. He'd prefer to have more time to do the things he loves, like playing tennis or a round of golf in the afternoon. Bob wants to slowly begin closing out his positions and transferring his funds into annuities. He likes the idea of not having to worry about market risk. Unfortunately, since September 2008, he's lost 50% or $7 million from his investment account. I'm mentioning Bob to make a point; Bob is a seasoned investor who was a successful hedge fund manager. Even with the benefit of his knowledge and expertise, he didn't see the market declining so significantly in 2008, or continue declining through the beginning of 2009. Interestingly enough, Bob did purchase several annuities before September of 2008. The annuities in Bob's financial portfolio were the only products in 2008, which made a profit.

Let's Consider the "Risk Factor" to Determine if the Risk Justifies the Gain

Expected rates of return compared to actual rates of return will result in two completely different values. All too often the expected rates of return evaporate into greed fueled hype. Is it worth taking such a high risk, with the possibility of significant market losses, for such a small yield spread between annuities and speculative investments?

When it comes to your investments, has your investment advisor ever given you this advice?

"The market is up… it's a good time to buy."

"The market is sideways…let's use dollar cost averaging to balance your financial portfolio."

"The market is down…this is a great time to buy and use dollar cost averaging to lower the overall cost of your investment positions."

"The market is down…hold on to your positions; remember what your original investment

objectives are and the time needed to accomplish your investment goals."

"The market is down significantly...Diversify, Diversify, and Diversify."

"The market is going to come back; if you sell your positions now, you're going to lose the gains and miss out on the recovery."

"It's only a loss if you sell."

Now let's have some fun using a "Rate of Return" comparison between Investments and Annuities.

Investment
Investment: $100,000.00
Rate of Return: 10% Annually
Account Balance after 10 years: $259,374.25
Market Correction: -35%
Account Balance after Correction: $168,593.26
Effective Yield for Investment: **6.85%**

Annuity
Annuity: $100,000.00
Rate of Return: 6% Compounding
Account Balance after 10 years: $179,084.77
Market Correction: 0%
Account Balance after Correction: $179,084.77
Effective Yield for Investment: **7.9%**

Investments and Annuities

Investments – Investments and investing is used in reference to securities such as stocks, bonds, and mutual funds. The downside of all investments is market risk and the inability to lock in the gains annually unless you sell, creating a taxable event.

Annuities – Annuities provide guarantees, tax deferred growth, and a triple compounding effect. Since annuities lock in the fixed rate of return each year, the compounding effect only increases the overall rate of return.

To keep it simple, securities offer investments and annuities offer guarantees.

When comparing the rate of return for investments vs. annuities the market does not move linearly, but in peaks and valleys. The previous illustration shows a 10% return for the investment and a 6% return for the annuity. The investment experienced a 35% decrease in the 10th year, which ultimately reduced the overall rate of return to 6.85%. As you can see, all market gains and losses will affect future market increases and declines and the overall rate of return. We experienced this when the market declined in 2000/2001 and again in 2008/2009. During both periods investors lost an average of 35% to 40% of their entire financial portfolio. How many investors were affected by the most recent declines in 2008/2009 that were in their retirement, close to retirement, or planned on retiring within a few years?

As you can see, the annuity offered a 6% rate of return, but the power of the annuity is two-fold. First, the annuity locks in the interest crediting rates each year and is applied to the balance. Second, the balance has the next years crediting interest rate applied to the account, compounding the interest to give an overall effective yield of 7.9% over the course of the last 10 years. This is using a basic fixed annuity to illustrate the power of *compound interest*.

What if it was possible to have an annuity linked to the S&P 500 Index®? A crediting option that would lock-in the gains each year the S&P® is up? In the years the S&P® is down, your account would be credited with zero, instead of the negative return from the S&P 500 Index®. This could be accomplished without any market risk. Does this sound too good to be true? It's not. It's available, and has been available for the last 15 years. It's just that no one has taken the time to tell you about it or explain to you how it works.

Today, there are many different annuities available with different crediting options. They include the S&P

500 Index®, DJIA®, Nasdaq 100®, and global strategies using a combination of several different indexes like the S&P 500 Index®, the Dow Jones EURO STOXX 50®, the Nikkei 225®, and the Hang Seng Index®, to name a few. This allows you to lock-in the gains, maximize your return, and without market risk.

As you can see, there certainly is a lot to choose from. It is a fixed annuity product and is known in the industry as fixed indexed annuity. Later, we will provide you with a complete breakdown of how fixed indexed annuities work and how you can benefit.

Just imagine how much more powerful the illustration would be if we compared the peaks and valleys of investments to the features and benefits of the fixed indexed annuity. Imagine having the ability to lock-in the gains each year from the S&P 500 Index® using fixed indexed annuities without any market risk. One of the biggest problems with investing is not having the ability to lock-in the gains each year, unless you sell your positions. With fixed indexed annuities, you can lock-in your gains each year, without any market risk and still have the power of compound interest. Not all fixed indexed annuities will allow you to annually lock-in your gains. Please make sure you understand your annuity contract and how it will be credited to your account and how frequently.

When a reporter asked Albert Einstein, *"What is the greatest invention of mankind?"* he responded, *"Compound Interest."* He was also quoted as saying: *"Compound Interest is the 8th Wonder or the World."* It certainly makes sense that a man who was known for being a great Mathematician, Scientist and Inventor was intrigued by the ability to continually compound a number to infinity.

Annuities and Your Financial Portfolio

We have finally made it to the point of discussing annuities and all the benefits associated with them. I hope you didn't mind taking a roundabout way of getting here. I just wanted to make sure you understood what has happened over the years, which lead us to where we are today. I believe, without this information, it would be difficult to understand the vital role annuities play in any financial portfolio. I want you to have the ability to make an informed decision concerning which annuity or annuities will work best for your particular situation. The possibilities are endless, so let's get started!

By now, I suppose you're beginning to understand there's a lot more to annuities than what you may have thought. I hear individuals say, *"Annuities are not for me!"* This tells me they spoke with someone who was not familiar with annuities, has limited knowledge and does not understand the financial benefits of annuities. Occasionally, someone will make a statement that they can receive a better return from the stock market than they can receive from annuities. As we discussed earlier, you may have a period of time when the performance of the market may provide a better rate of return than an annuity, but what happens in the negative years and how does that affect the overall effective yield of your financial portfolio? Annuities are steady, offer a good rate of return, and will achieve your desired result without any market risk. As we compared investment vs. annuities in the previous chapter, a decreasing market diminishes the overall rate of return from the investment since you do not have the ability to lock-in the gains, without selling the position. Annuities have the ability to lock-in crediting rates, typically on an annual basis regardless of market performance.

Today, we are hearing a lot about capital reserve issues in the financial services industry. The federal government provided funds to banking institutions to ease the credit markets and to shore up the banks' financial balance sheets so they could begin lending money again. Unfortunately, banking institutions are retaining the funds to improve or maintain their own capital reserve requirements. Even though insurance companies have the same capital reserve requirements as banks, annuities, unlike securities (unless you have a variable annuity with the income benefit rider, which is contractually guaranteed), must reserve the capital required to meet their financial obligations, which are contractually guaranteed to protect the policy holders. This includes rate guarantees, minimum rate guarantees, income guarantees, and living benefit guarantees. If you have an annuity, which offers an income benefit rider, the value of the annuity to provide the guaranteed income benefit is contractual and must be reserved. Even the life only income must be reserved for the life expectancy of the annuitant or client.

I am surprised at how many individuals relate annuities to income only and not as a resource that offers safety, security and guarantees. There are many different types of annuities with many variations in the way they work, the benefits available, riders, options, income, tax deferral, and so on. So, let's break it all down so you can understand the advantages of using annuities.

The Benefits of Using Annuities

Income - Annuities can provide you with an income if you have the need and choose to pursue it. There are two categories. Your funds will either be classified as tax-qualified or non-qualified funds, which will determine the taxation of the income you receive.

Tax-Qualified – These are funds from IRA, 401(k) Plans, SEP Plans, Simple IRA, 412(i) Plans, Defined Benefit Plans, etc. This includes any and all funds you received as a deduction (in any given year), and have been identified to the IRS as funds for your future retirement. All qualified funds are 100% taxable.

Non-Qualified – These are funds that have previously been taxed. Since these funds are after-tax dollars, they are referred to as having the original principal or a cost basis. You only pay taxes on the future gains and interest above and beyond your original principal deposit or cost basis.

Immediate Annuities – This is a contractual agreement designed specifically for income purposes only. The income must begin within 12 months to be classified as an immediate annuity. If the annuity does not begin to generate an income until after 12 months, you cannot use an immediate annuity, but instead must use a deferred annuity with a provision to convert to an immediate annuity for income at a future point in time. The payouts options may vary, so it is important to use a company that offer specific terms for your financial situation.

It is important to realize, once you have elected an income stream from an immediate annuity or converted from a deferred annuity contract, the annuity contract is considered annuitized. You forfeit any and all future rights to the original deposit and/or the remaining account balance.

The following are the most common immediate annuity options available. Please do not assume all companies offer each and every option:

Life Only – This option is most often used when there is no surviving spouse. For married couples, choosing a joint life income could reduce the income payout by as much as 50% of their retirement income. Instead, they can choose a life only payout for the maximum retirement income and purchase a life insurance policy to provide the income stream for the surviving spouse for pennies on the dollar. This is a good example of using annuities with life insurance, also known as arbitrage.

This option refers to an income annuity which will pay a specific amount over the lifetime of a single individual, known as the annuitant. This is also the highest payout for an annuity income structure. As an example, a female who is currently 65 years of age and has a life expectancy of 22 years (or is expected to live until age 87), could expect an income of $1,000 per month. If she lives for only 10 years, the income stops immediately. If she continues to live until age 100, the income will continue for as long as she lives.

Joint Life – This is a 100% payout based upon

the life expectancy of both individuals and will continue to payout for as long as each individual is living. Upon the death of either annuitant, the income will remain the same and continue until the second annuitant is deceased. Even though the income is based upon both life expectancies, it is the younger of the two individuals, which determines the payout schedule. This is a standard immediate annuity option used when both annuitants are close in age.

Joint Survivorship Life – This option reduces the income benefit payout based upon the death of either annuitant. In many cases, both individuals are willing to receive a payout based upon a joint life schedule with a future reduction based upon the death of either annuitant. The reduction is typically 50% to 75% of the original joint life income payment schedule.

There are normally two reasons why a couple will choose this option:

The income reduction for either annuitant will not change or affect the surviving spouse's standard of living or quality of life.

There is an age difference of 10 or more years which negatively effects the payout option for a joint life schedule.

This option can be a double-edged sword. As

an example: An annuitant age 70 years of age, converts $500,000 from their 401(k) to purchase an immediate annuity. The spouse is 60 years of age and they choose a joint survivorship life option with a 50% reduction upon the death of either annuitant. The monthly payout is $3,000 while they are both living. A year later, the spouse dies at the age of 61. The income for the surviving annuitant reduces to $1,500 per month for as long as the annuitant is living. In this case scenario, even though an individual loves their spouse and mourns the loss, it would still be a very costly endeavor. This is standard with most insurance companies and their payouts under the provisions of a joint survivorship life contract.

On the other hand, another option which is generally not known by financial professionals or offered by insurance companies is the ability under the Joint Survivorship Life contract to identify a primary and secondary annuitant. What makes this option so appealing is when a married couple has an age difference of 10 or more years. The reduction can be applied to the death of the primary annuitant only, not based upon the death of the secondary annuitant. As an example: using the same scenario with the primary annuitant age 70 and the spouse age 60 (the secondary annuitant) and receive $3,000 per month. The income benefit will be reduced to $1,500 per month upon the death of the primary annuitant only. If the secondary annuitant predeceases the primary annuitant, the income benefit remains the same at $3,000 per month. It is important to remember, since most financial professionals are unaware of this option, it must be requested.

Period Certain – This is an income stream that is designed to payout for a period certain and then all income stops. Normally, the options for income are for 5-year period certain, 10-year period certain to as much as 20-year period certain. As an example, if an individual chose a 10-year period certain, regardless of how long the individual lives, the income would stop after 10 years. If the individual becomes deceased in year six, the income would continue to the beneficiary for the remainder of the guaranteed period certain payout. In this case, the payments would continue for four more years for a total contractual payout of 10 years.

Life with Period Certain – This payout option combines the benefits of a life only payout with a period certain payout. As an example: if you choose life with 10-year period certain, it will provide a payout for as long as the client lives. If the client is currently 65 and lived until age 100, the income would be guaranteed to continue paying the income benefit for the life of the annuitant, regardless of how long they live. If the client were to become deceased at the age of 72, or seven years into the annuity contract, the payments would continue for three additional years for a total payout of 10 years. Contractually, it works the same for a life and 20-year period certain.

Life with Cash Refund Option – This option will pay the annuitant for as long as they shall live. If they were to die prematurely or before the entire account value is liquidated, the balance of the funds would be paid directly to the named beneficiary.

Age Rated or Medically Underwritten Immediate Annuities – There are very few insurance companies who still offer medically underwritten immediate annuities today. The insurance company will have an underwriter and/ or possibly a medical director who reviews the medical records. Based upon the information, the client's life expectancy may be reduced. As an example, a 70-year-old female, has a normal life expectancy of age 87 and the payout would be $1,000 per month on a life only basis. Due to her medical conditions, her true life expectancy may be 82. With the life expectancy reduced from 87 to age 82, which is 5 years less than normal. The insurance company agrees to pay $1,350 monthly on a life only basis. The payout is higher based upon the reduced or shorter life expectancy of the client.

Structured Settlement – A structured settlement is normally court ordered or is agreed to by both parties and accepted by the judge assigned to the case in the judicial system. As the name implies, it is a settlement amount that is structured to pay out over a period of time, but is typically paid out over the lifetime of an individual. As an example: the court ordered a specific payout of $100,000 per year, for the care of an individual over their lifetime, but medically the life expectancy is 10 years. The sum of $1,000,000 is deposited and begins to pay out $100,000 each year over the total life expectancy or for a 10 year period. The problem is the individual could live beyond 10 years and the account would be liquidated without any future income.

If the court ordered a structured settlement in the amount of $100,000 a year, for as long as the individual shall live, knowing that the life expectancy is approximately 10 years, an insurance company agrees to provide an immediate annuity costing $850,000 and agrees to payout the $100,000 per year for the life of the individual. The insurance company believes medically that the individual's life expectancy is 8 years, not the 10 years previously estimated. If the insurance company is right, they can make a profit of $150,000; if they're wrong, it could cost the insurance company hundreds of thousands of dollars.

Regardless of the cost, insurance companies know how to evaluate risk and they apply the same rules using dollar cost averaging by evaluating and structuring hundreds and thousands of immediate annuities for the structured settlement industry. The judge, attorneys, and family members would all be in agreement, knowing the individual will be financially secure through their entire life expectancy. There is approximately $150,000 savings by using an immediate annuity from the original $1,000,000 deposit.

Not all insurance companies are equal with respect to their immediate annuity payout rates. It is important to have an annuity specialist who can provide you with the most competitive payout rates available. Any annuity specialist should have access to at least 25 insurance companies, if not more, and provide you with top three payout rates for you to choose from. The numbers are constantly changing, so you can never assume that a company, who has the best payout rates today, will be the best tomorrow.

The Most & Least Common Options for Income

Life with 10-Year Period Certain – This is the most common choice, since this contract ensures the entire account value would be paid out to the annuitant or to their beneficiaries, regardless of the life expectancy of the client.

Life with 20-Year Period Certain – This is not the most popular option since it pays the least amount of income. However, it is guaranteed to pay out for the longest period of time.

Life with Cash Refund – This is a popular option but doesn't have the best pay out rates. This is for the individual who wants to ensure that the money not used in the contract goes to a named beneficiary, which is paid out upon death.

Life Only – This option has the highest payout option available. It is also directly related to the 10-year bond rate. Upon execution, the immediate annuity contract will lock in a guaranteed payout for the life of the individual. This also includes joint life and joint survivorship life.

Immediate annuity quotes will be guaranteed to hold the rate for normally 7 to 10 days. If you choose an immediate annuity, be conscious of the 10-year bond rate. Should the 10-year bond rate increase while you are waiting for your policy to be issued, you can request the higher payout if the bond rate goes up. If you have an annuity specialist, he/she should know this information and will work on your behalf to ensure you always receive the best payout rates available.

We have covered so much about annuities thus far, but it's only been about immediate annuities and the payout options and alternatives available. I'm sure at this point you're asking yourself, "*So, what's the big deal? It provides an income. I can get an income anywhere. What makes an immediate annuity so special?*" Here's where the rubber meets the road with annuities. Tax-qualified funds are 100% taxable. Unfortunately, we can't do anything about that. However, non-qualified funds have a cost basis, meaning that a percentage of the funds have already paid tax on the principal. Non-qualified funds deposited into an immediate annuity are classified as a return of premium and the tax liability is spread out over the life of the contract. There is also an exclusion ratio that excludes a percentage of the income you receive from being taxed. For example, if you were receiving $1,000 of monthly income and you have an exclusion ratio of 86%, you would only pay taxes on $140 of the monthly income you receive. The balance of the income would be classified as a refund of premium. With any other vehicle, all gains and interest would require 100% of the proceeds to be taxed first, before you receive your original principal.

Deferred Annuities – As previously mentioned, immediate annuities are for income purposes only. Deferred annuities cover every aspect, including all future income needs, options, and alternatives from the previous section. The difference is an immediate annuity must begin income payments within 12 months from the contract date. Deferred annuities were created for growth and tax deferral. You only begin to pay tax once you begin taking a distribution on your funds. They can be converted to an income stream at a future point in time to mitigate the tax liability over your lifetime. Remember, annuities are for safety, security, and guarantees. Income is just one of the many benefits annuities can provide to you and only if needed.

There are many different types of annuities designed to accomplish many different objectives, whether you are trying to maximize your return or provide a guaranteed rate of return for a specific period of time, or to simply create a safe money solution. Please keep in mind that all safe money solutions should provide you with complete accessibility to your total account value. There are also many different types of riders which allow full access to your funds during the surrender charge period. Refer to your specific policy or the annuity information (you are thinking about purchasing) to see what provisions of the contract allow for partial or full accessibility.

It is not uncommon for an annuity policy holder to

have several different annuities from several different companies within their financial portfolio. Annuities are designed to meet different needs and objectives. Using the surrender charge periods, guarantee periods, and crediting methods can clearly create a well-balance financial portfolio.

Let's go over the intricacies of an annuity, so you understand the various elements and aspects of annuities and how they relate to you:

Surrender Charge – All annuity policies have a surrender charge period. Each surrender charge period is different from one annuity to the next. There are some annuities which let you choose how long of a surrender charge you would like to have. Can you believe it? Others may tell you annuities limit access to your funds or have long surrender charge periods. Now you know better. There are so many options and alternatives available that any annuity specialist should be able to find the right annuity to meet your needs, goals, and objectives within your own specific timeline.

It is important to determine which surrender charge period is right for you and meets your goals, objectives, and most importantly, are within your timeline. Also, look at the riders available in the contract. It could be your "Get Out of Jail Free" card. As an example, some policies will allow you to transfer your funds if the interest rates fall below a certain threshold. Let's say the base rate or the threshold is 3% and interest rates fall below the 3% mark. You will automatically be able to transfer your funds to another company free of any surrender charges.

Guarantee Periods – Many insurance companies offer a guarantee period. You have to be very careful with these products, since they're not as straight forward as other annuity products. *This product offers a guaranteed rate of return for a specific period of time, but the surrender charge period is longer than the rate guarantee period.* This is a completely different product from a MYG (Multi-Year Guarantee) product. I do like the MYG products as long as the surrender charge period matches the guarantee rate period.

Timeline – What is your time horizon? Are the funds going to be used as a part of your retirement plan? At what age do you plan on retiring? Are the funds tax-qualified or non-qualified? All of these questions and more need to be addressed. This is very important to determine the length and type of investment or which annuity is right for you and your financial portfolio.

New Money, Old Money, & Portfolio Rates – Be aware that there are insurance companies, which offer different rates based upon whether the policy holder is currently a client or a prospective client who will deposit or transfer new money to the insurance company.

New Money Rates – As with any other business, in a capitalistic society, even insurance companies need to attract new business. New money rates are one way insurance companies entice new customers by offering better than average rates of return for new depositors.

For your information, all funds either deposited or transferred to an insurance company are considered new money. One of the most noticeable differences for new money is with immediate annuity rates. For example, if you currently have funds in an annuity and you wish to annuitize the contract for a life income payout, the rate would be less with your current company than what you would receive from a new company. By transferring your funds from your previous insurance company, you would receive the new money rate, which offers a higher payout.

Old Money Rates – There is definitely a difference between new money and old money rates. If you currently have an annuity with a particular insurance company, don't be surprised to find the rate you received is lower than the new money rate being offered for new clients. It is not uncommon for the current rate or crediting rate to be lower. This is the reason why an annuity specialist will continuously evaluate your annuity and make recommendations for changes when you have the opportunity to increase the overall rate of return on your financial portfolio.

Portfolio Rate – The difference between the old money rate and new money rate in most cases can be attributed to the portfolio rate, but not in all cases. For the past 20 years, the financial industry has been in a decreasing interest rate environment. The lower interest rates have affected the overall rate of return, reducing the value of the entire financial portfolio. Instead of diminishing the rate of return further, insurance companies will close out their portfolio by not accepting any new contributions or additional funds.

The insurance company will begin a *new* portfolio, based upon the rates available from the new investment portfolio. This will happen over and over again as rates continue to decrease. As interest rates increase, they will continue to close out old portfolios and open new portfolios to receive higher rates of return to attract new funds for deposits.

The following is an example of a Portfolio Rate:

Year Open	Year Closed	Portfolio No.	Overall Rate
1995	1998	1	8.75%
1998	2001	2	6.48%
2001	2005	3	5.10%
2005	2007	4	4.10%
2007	OPEN	5	5.00%

This is a simplistic illustration to show you the different portfolio rates within an insurance company's financial portfolio. The financial portfolio and how long the client has been in the financial portfolio of the insurance company will determine their crediting or current interest rate. This is how one client can receive a better rate of return than another client with the same insurance company but with different financial portfolios.

Multi-Year Guaranteed Annuity (MYG) – This is

one of the most popular annuities. It guarantees a rate of return for a specific period of time. Everyone knows exactly what the guaranteed rate is, how long it will last, and when the rate stops or is no longer guaranteed. You can choose between 3, 5, 6, 8, & 10 years with a guaranteed rate. These are the most popular options, but there are many other options available.

This is how a typical MYG product works: If you decided to choose a 5-year guaranteed annuity with a 5% guaranteed rate of return, the chassis of the annuity is normally a 7 to 10 year surrender charge period. At the end of the guaranteed period (in this case, 5 years), you normally have a 30-day penalty free window to renew for another guaranteed period, transfer your funds to another company, or receive the current crediting interest rate declared annually for the balance of the surrender charge period.

Market Value Adjustment (MVA) – You should be aware of MVA (Market Value Adjustment) products and how they work. They have the ability to increase or decrease your account value after the guaranteed rate of return term has ended and the funds are transferred. Not all companies or states allow for MVA products, but you should be aware if the product you are purchasing is, in fact, an MVA product.

This is how it works: If you have a guaranteed rate of return or current interest rate for your policy and the rate you're receiving is greater than the current interest rates available for new money, the cash value in your policy increases. If the guaranteed rate of return or current interest rates from your policy remain the same, but is less than the current crediting interest rate for new money, your account value will decrease.

It sounds confusing and it is. However, you need to be aware of the MVA process so you can understand why your account value went up or down, after you transferred the funds from your policy, within the allowable 30-day window, following the end of your guaranteed rate of return period.

Fixed Indexed Annuities

This product was first introduced approximately 10 years ago. This is by far the most innovative product design, one that had a huge impact across the entire financial services industry. It would be comparable to the impact universal life policies had on traditional whole life policies, or how term insurance affected universal life policies today.

What makes fixed indexed annuities so incredible? It's the ability to have a single product, which offers a guaranteed minimum interest rate to protect your principal, a crediting rate linked to the performance of an index or indices (such as the S&P 500 Index®) to create maximum growth potential, and the capability to accomplish these results without any market risk. I used the term index and also indices. Both are appropriate and correct terms in the financial services industry.

Before I describe the basics of a fixed indexed

annuity, I would like to make it perfectly clear that your funds are never invested in the market. I am going to repeat this one more time: *Your funds are never invested in the market.* If you purchase a fixed indexed annuity product and agree to accept a lower minimum guaranteed interest rate, based upon a lower percentage of your original deposit, the insurance company will provide you with an opportunity to participate in the performance of the general account fund of the insurance company.

As I previously explained, all guarantees offered by insurance companies must be reserved. If the guarantees of the original deposit and guaranteed minimum interest rates are contractually lower, it allows more funds to be transferred to the general account fund of the insurance company for purchasing options, instead of being used for capital reserves. The insurance companies purchase options on indexes or indices. For example, based upon the S&P 500 Index®, the cost to purchase indexed options would be pennies on the dollar. Normally, the indexed options will remain valid for one year. At the end of one year, the indexed option has either made money or expired worthless. The loss is limited to the original cost of the indexed option only. If the S&P 500 Index® was down for the year and the indexed option expired worthless, your account would be credited with zero, not the negative reflected in the S&P 500 Index®. If the S&P 500 Index® finished the year with a gain, your account would be credited with the percentage of the gain based upon your fixed indexed annuity and the crediting indexed option you chose. The indexed option would be linked to your annuity's participation rate, cap rate, and yield spread or a combination of the three.

There are some annuity products that purchase indexed options with an expiration date 10 years in the future. Since the insurance company knows the cost of the indexed options purchased with a 10-year expiration date, they can afford to offer a 100% participation rate, no cap rate, and no yield spread, without any future changes, making this contractual within the policy, and passing the advantages on to you.

With most insurance companies who purchase indexed options for a 1-year or 2-year timeline, it is impossible to know the future cost of the indexed option. Insurance companies use participation rates, cap rates, and yield spreads to control the future cost of the indexed options.

What gives fixed indexed annuities the power they have in the financial services industry? There are three features that make fixed indexed annuities stand far above the rest compared to any other financial service products: 1) the ability to provide guarantees, 2) the ability to maximize your return using indexing as a crediting method, and 3) the ability to lock-in the gains each year, if possible, compounding the interest to receive a triple compounding affect on your funds.

Indexed Crediting Options – As stated earlier, crediting options for fixed indexed annuities are used to help insurance companies control the future cost of the index crediting options. The crediting options are available in various forms as participation rates, cap rates, and yield spreads. The costs of purchasing indexed crediting options for fixed indexed annuities are controlled by supply and demand only. If the cost of the indexed crediting options becomes too expensive, you defeat the purpose of purchasing options unless you have alternatives available to you, which help give you control of the cost of the options that may be purchased. For example, last year insurance companies purchased fixed indexed annuity options, which offered a 100% participation rate. The cost of the same option today is twice the price, but you can purchase an 80% participation rate for the same price as last year's rate. In this example, if you are paying a higher price for the same option, instead of maximizing your return, you ultimately reduced your return; due to the higher cost paid to purchase the same options from one year ago. In other words, you spent more money, received fewer options, and reduced your overall rate of return.

Participation Rates – Many fixed indexed annuity contracts use participation rates to control future cost of the indexing options. The fixed indexed annuity contract will provide any and all information regarding the lowest participation rate available.

The following demonstrates how the participation rate works within a fixed indexed annuity contract: Assume we are using the S&P 500 Index® as the crediting option, the S&P 500 Index® had a 20%

return for the year, and the current participation rate is 80%. The 20% rate of return from the S&P 500 Index® would receive 80% as the participation rate. The total percentage credited to the fixed indexed annuity is a 16% rate of return for the year.

Performance of S&P 500 Index®: +20%
Crediting Participation Rate: 80%
Actual Indexed Crediting: +16%

As you can see, you may not receive the full account value of the S&P 500 Index®, but you received a nice return without any market risk.

Cap Rates – The cap rate for fixed indexed annuities is very similar to the participation rate. It is very easy to understand because the maximum return is limited to the cap rate, which is contractually offered by the insurance company. The annuity contract will provide any and all information concerning the highest or lowest cap rate available within the annuity contract. The cap rate limitations will normally reflect both the lowest to the highest cap rate available contractually.

The following demonstrates how the cap rate works within an fixed indexed annuity contract: Assume we are using the S&P 500 Index® as the crediting option, the S&P 500® had a 20% return for the year, and the current cap rate was limited to 16% maximum. Therefore, out of the 20% the S&P 500 Index® received, only 16% would be credited to the fixed indexed annuity for a total return of 16% for the year.

Performance of S&P 500 Index®: +20%
Crediting Cap Rate: 16%
Actual Indexed Crediting: +16%

Again, as you can see, you may not receive the full account value of the S&P 500 Index®, but you received a nice return without any market risk.

Yield Spread – There are many individuals who interpret yield spread as an asset management fee. It works the exact same way as an asset management fee, but not all fixed indexed annuities have a yield spread, so I do not classify it as a true asset management fee. The fixed indexed annuity contract will provide any and all information concerning the yield spread and disclose the maximum charge for the yield spread annually and may fluctuate throughout the term of the annuity contract.

Performance of S&P 500 Index®: +20%
Crediting Yield Spread: - 4%
Actual Indexed Crediting: +16%

Finally, as you can see, you may not receive the full account value of the S&P 500 Index®, but you received a nice return without any market risk.

Current Crediting Interest Rates – The current crediting interest rates for fixed indexed annuities have nothing to do with indexes, participation rates, yield spreads, cap rates, or guaranteed minimum interest rates. It has to do with the current interest rate that the fixed indexed annuity will credit to your account if you choose this option.

Due to our current financial crisis and the low interest rate environment that has occurred for the past 15 years, I believe interest rates are going to significantly increase in the future. Many individuals overlook fixed rates of return. However, there was a time during the 80's when you could receive interest rates as high as 15% guaranteed for 5 years. I'm mentioning this to you so you keep your eye on future interest rates. If we reach a point when we can receive a current interest rate of 8% or higher, it's my recommendation to lock in the rate as soon as possible, for as long as possible.

Guaranteed Minimum Interest Rates – With fixed indexed annuities, the average guarantee is based upon 87.5% to 100% of the original deposit. The guaranteed minimum interest rate is .50% to as much as 3% annually. The following demonstrates how the minimum guaranteed interest rate is 2.5% and is based upon 87.5% of the original deposit with a 10-year surrender charge period for a fixed indexed annuity.

Original Deposit: $ 100,000.00
Guaranteed Crediting: 87.50%
Guaranteed Account Value: $87,500.00
Minimum Guaranteed Interest Rate: 2.50%
Account Value after 10 Years: $112,007.40

This is based upon the minimum guarantees within the fixed indexed annuity contract until the surrender charge period has been satisfied and no withdrawals have been taken from the policy. This is the worst case scenario. In order to receive the minimum guarantees contractually, the current interest rate must fall below the minimum guaranteed rate in the contract. The index must have a negative return for the next 10 years, crediting the indexed account with zero for your fixed indexed annuity annually. Is it worth having a fixed indexed annuity, which offers a minimum guaranteed interest rate, with the ability to maximize your return, and accomplish this without any market risk? I think so, and so do thousands of clients who have moved literally billions of dollars into fixed indexed annuities annually for the last 10 years.

Surrender Charges – All annuities have surrender charges. It doesn't matter if it's a variable, fixed indexed, or a deferred annuity; they all have surrender charges. They vary in penalty fees or percentages charged for early termination of the annuity contract. Always read all of the information concerning the annuity you plan to purchase, so you are not surprised down the road. It's difficult to use the excuse that you didn't read or understand the provisions of the contract after you have held the policy for 10 years.

The surrender charges will vary with annuities beginning with as little as 3 years, to as much as a 20-year surrender charge period. Naturally, you purchase an annuity contract based upon your time horizon. If you are in your late 30's, having a contract with a 15-year surrender charge period would have very little effect on you. As always, you would want the annuity to provide a good rate of return, and meet your goals and objectives for your financial portfolio.

Bonuses – There are many fixed indexed annuities that offer a first year bonus. A few companies will give you bonuses on additional funds deposited, up to the fifth year. If you combine it with first year interest rate, you can end up with a very nice first year rate of return or a nice effective yield over the term of the annuity contract.

Here is an example using the first year rate with a first year bonus: The initial deposit is $100,000 and receives a 10% bonus of $10,000. The account balance is now $110,000. The first year interest rate is 3.75%. This brings the total first year account balance to $114,125 providing an effective yield of 14.12% at the end of the first year. See the following illustration:

First Year Deposit: $100,000.00
First Year Bonus: 10%
First Year Current Fixed Rate: 3.75%
Account Value after 1ˢᵗ Year: $114,125.00
First Year Yield: 14.12%
5 Year Yield at Current Rate: 5.83%
Account Value after 5 Years: $132,230.98

This was accomplished using only current interest rates. It was not linked to the S&P 500 Index® or any other indices and was still accomplished without any market risk. Being able to receive a 5.83% return for the next 5 years, without any market risk, is incredible by today's standards. Although I am using current interest rates, if I used the minimum guaranteed rate of 2.10%, which is contractually guaranteed, you would still receive 4.43% for the next 5 years. No matter how you slice it, dice it, or chop it up, it's still a decent return in today's market.

Even though a fixed indexed annuity offers a bonus, some insurance companies will apply the bonus on the first day, as if it were deposited into the account when the policy was issued. Other insurance companies will add the bonus to the policy at the end of the first year. There are a few companies that provide a bonus, which is applied to your account on the first day, but has a vesting schedule over a period of time before it is free and clear in your account. You just need to be aware how the bonus is applied to your policy and how it will work, in order to receive the full benefits of the bonus for your financial portfolio.

Liquidity – I do not believe anyone should get into a fixed indexed annuity contract with the thought of accessing cash from the policy prior to the end of the surrender charge period, other than in the case of an emergency. The only other acceptable situation is using the income benefit rider for a higher guaranteed income benefit. Even though these policies have provisions for withdrawals, I do not advise anyone to enter into a contractual agreement with that thought it mind.

I do understand situations will arise when accessibility may be needed due to a particular situation or circumstance, beyond anyone's control. Make sure your policy allows for this type of provision, which will allow you to access a portion, if not all, of your account value, in case of emergencies and/or medical conditions or financial uncertainty.

Under normal circumstances, you can access the interest only or up to 10% of the cash accumulation value in your policy. However, be aware not all policies provide access to your account value without incurring a surrender charge. Some insurance companies will provide access up to 10% of the original deposit only, not the full cash accumulation value.

As with any other product in your financial portfolio, annuities are no different and should be evaluated and reviewed annually. If you are using indexing to maximize your return, great! Recently, there have been many financial analysts speculating that our economy will experience hyper inflation in the near future. If this happens, we could potentially see interest rates skyrocket to double digit returns; similar to what we experienced in the 1980's.

If interest rates reach 8% or higher, I would recommend each individual to take 100% of their funds from their fixed annuity or fixed indexed annuity policy and place it in the current fixed interest rate account only. Unless you review your account annually, you may not know that the interest rates have increased and you may miss the opportunity to receive a higher rate of return by using the current fixed interest rates, instead of using index crediting options to maximize your return.

Living Benefits & Annuities

As our aging population retires, the greatest fear isn't dying prematurely; it's outliving our retirement income. Further compounding the issue is the fact that we are living longer, but not necessarily healthier.

These are the major concerns for individuals who are currently in retirement or soon to be retired:

THE RETIREMENT FACTOR:

Outliving your income or nest egg

Cost of prescription drugs

Quality of medical care in retirement

Future increases in income taxes

I don't know of any other products that offer additional benefits comparable to what annuities offer today. Annuities offer you a guaranteed rate of return (or fixed indexed annuities that have the ability to maximize your return without any market risk), tax deferral, compound interest, guaranteed income (should you need it), or you can use a income benefit rider, without annuitizing the contract for income, and finally, living benefits which could be significantly greater than your total account value.

What living benefits are being offered through your bank, P&C agencies, or from your investment firms? This is just another example of how important it is to diversify to create a well-balanced financial portfolio. Yes, it is important to invest, just as it is important to preserve and protect. As I have stated previously, I'm not opposed to investing. I'm just opposed to any individual who promotes diversification as being limited only to the investment industry and does not include safe money solutions with guarantees.

THE NEED FACTOR:

Over 700,000 strokes a Year, 28% under 65 yrs. old

Over 60,000 new cases of Parkinson's annually; average onset 60 yrs. old

Every 29 seconds, someone has a coronary event

Alzheimer patients diagnosed before age 65 accounts for 6% to 10% of all cases

70% of people over age 65 will need some type of

long term care within their lifetime

The financial services crisis of 2008/2009 has had a huge impact on our economy, and will affect us financially for years to come. We are currently at a 10% unemployment rate, which is expected to increase. We also have the highest foreclosure rate in the history of our country. To further compound the problems, the government is receiving less in revenues, which will have a dramatic impact on future services previously provided.

THE REALITY FACTOR:

2017 - More money is paid out from Social Security than the government is receiving

2018 - Medicaid becomes bankrupt

2040 - Social Security becomes bankrupt

The ugly truth is that the dates used above are incorrect. The high unemployment numbers, which continue to rise each and every month, has impacted the revenues the federal government receives. These are federally funded programs and the truth of the matter is, no one has current data to determine the actual dates when these programs will run out of money. But they do know it will be a lot sooner due to the state of the economy compared to what was previously projected.

Even though you have paid into the Social Security System for years, who's going to pay for your future care? Unfortunately, the reality factor may come down to your own financial resources. Many of us cannot afford to wait for the economy to recover and need to find other options and alternatives today. This is the reason why I believe the living benefits may be one of the best financial tools within our arsenal or products to be used.

Activities of Daily Living (ADL) – The activities of daily living will have the most direct impact for increasing living benefits. Activities of daily living are defined as: The ability to perform daily activities on your own accord to maintain or enhance one's quality of life. This includes such activities as eating, bathing, dressing, transferring, toileting, and continence, which requires you to accomplish these tasks on your own and unassisted.

Living Benefits – Recently, I called an insurance company to find out more about their particular living benefits that they offered through their annuity contracts. A marketing representative told me that they do not offer living benefits on their annuity contracts and that they are only available on their life products. I re-phrased the question and asked again, *"Will your annuity products allow for an increase in monthly benefits if an individual is unable to complete 2 of 6 activities of daily living (ADL)?"* She responded, *"Yes, but that's not a living benefit, that is an option available as part of an income benefit rider with our annuities."*

Home office personnel may not have the years of experience or understand the questions you may be asking. Policies are designed with specific objectives in mind. The maximum growth potential may be your first objective, but 30 years from now, you may want to convert that policy to provide an income. The income the policy provides is a living benefit. This is an additional benefit, which is only available to you while you are living. If you have the opportunity to increase the payout rate due to your inability to complete 2 of 6 activities of daily living (ADL), the additional benefit would be classified as a living benefit since it increases the monthly income payout rates. If you were in a situation needing to stay in a long term care facility, many policies will provide full access, increase access, and may increase the income stream significantly based upon your life expectancy. Depending upon your age, these living benefits may not be important to you. However, if you are older or looking toward the future, you may want to consider what options and alternatives are available to you, using annuities for additional living benefits.

There are more policies being designed, which provide living benefits within annuities. This is just in case you need access due to unforeseen medical conditions in the future. Many times, you will find the living benefits may far outweigh the full account value accrued over time. The living benefits are normally linked directly to activities of daily living (ADL) and can increase your monthly payout to provide an additional monetary benefit for you and for the care you need.

Let's look at how the living benefit to enhance the income payout based upon the inability to perform 2 or more activities of daily living (ADL): In this example, we have a 65-year old female, who decides to use the guaranteed income benefit rider. Her original deposit was $100,000. She does not want to completely annuitize her annuity contract, but wants to supplement her retirement income since she has a good retirement income from her job and the additional income she receives from Social Security.

CURRENTLY HAS THE ABILITY TO PERFORM ALL 6 ADL:
Female Retirement Age: 65
Current Annual Income: $7,012.00

At age 67, she can no longer perform 2 of the 6 activities of daily living (ADL). She decides to execute the income benefit rider from her annuity contract to begin receiving an additional annual income.

After 2 years, she can no longer perform 2 or more of the 6 activities of daily living and the income benefit increases:

Current Retirement Age: 67
Total Annuity Account Value: $113,118.00
Enhanced Benefit: x 8.7%
Annual Income increased to: $9,698.00

As you can see, there is a lot more to annuities than what you may have expected. An annuity specialist can help assist you in choosing the right annuity for you. One that can provide accessibility and living benefits that could be beneficial for your financial portfolio. Perhaps your objective is having an annuity to help assist you in recovering from previous market losses, or using the annuity to create a safe money solution. Maybe it's to provide you with a guaranteed income stream without annuitizing the annuity contract through the use of the income benefit rider. There are over 2,500 insurance companies and over 1,000 annuities being offered...*which one is the right annuity for you?*

Riders and Additional "Living Benefits" for Annuities

All riders are separate from the annuity contract. There is normally a cost associated with them, which must be paid on an annual basis. It is automatically deducted from the cash value of the annuity policy. Under certain circumstances, the insurance company may add the riders automatically to new annuity policies. In some situations, they will make the rider retroactively available to any and all existing policy holders at no additional cost.

If you are working with an annuity specialist, make sure they explain the options and alternatives available to you through the provisions and additional riders of the annuity contract.

Income Benefit Rider – Insurance companies like to have everything copywritten, including their marketing materials, their various products brochures and their living benefit riders. The living benefit riders have different names and may be referred to as a guaranteed income benefit rider, the lifetime income benefit rider, or the lifetime income guaranteed rider; all income benefit riders are basically the same. I like making things simple. Because we are discussing the rider in general, I am going to use the term income benefit rider, which refers to all riders that provide a lifetime income benefit without annuitizing.

This is an incredible rider, which has been used by many clients recently to make up for market losses of 2008/2009, especially from their retirement account. When you can show someone how to re-coup market losses and receive the retirement income they were expecting to receive, that's pretty incredible. Even though it is a paper gain used only as the basis to determine or establish the income to be generated for retirement, it's still a nice option to have. The fee for this rider can be as little as 0% or as much as .60% basis points annually.

Today, many insurance companies automatically include the income benefit rider at no additional cost. Typically, it offers 5% compounding contractually and is based upon the original deposit of the annuity. If you wish to receive a higher compounding rate than what is offered to you at no cost, you can receive as much as 8% rate of return, compounding contractually for 10 years for an additional fee of .45% annually. If you were not planning to retire or receive an income for at least 10 years, it would easily justify the cost because the income would be so much greater.

The policy will contractually guarantee a client a specific income based upon a guaranteed rate of return (the average is 6%; however, there are fixed indexed annuity companies offering a 12% bonus with 8% compounding contractually for 10 years), regardless of market performance. Should the account value increase, your income stream will receive the higher income or step-up in income based upon the increase of the account value. Here is an example of how the income benefit rider can benefit you and your financial portfolio:

Let's say Joe is a high level executive who has lost 50% of his retirement account since September of 2008. He is currently 60 years of age and was expecting to retire at age 65. He decided to purchase an annuity, which offers the income benefit rider with a 12% bonus immediately beginning on the first day, compounding contractually at 8% annually.

BEGINNING ACCOUNT VALUE: $500,000.00
12% First Year Bonus: $60,000.00
Compounding Rate Annually: 8%
First Year End Account Value: $604,800.00

JOE DECIDES TO RETIRE AT THE END OF HIS 5TH YEAR:
Account Value after 5 years: $822,823.72
Guaranteed Income Annually: $41,141.19

If Joe decided to retire after the 8th year, he would have recovered to total account value for income purposes only.

Account Value after 8 years: $1,036,520.92
Guaranteed Income Annually: $51,826.05

With the income benefit rider, the income illustrated above is 100% contractually guaranteed. The income generated from the income benefit rider can be executed at any time without incurring a surrender charge. In reference to taxation on the proceeds, if the funds are tax-qualified from a retirement account, the funds would automatically be taxed 100%. If the funds are non-qualified and had an original cost basis, and the annuity contract is not being annuitized, all income will still be taxed 100%. Upon reaching the original cost basis, the funds would then be classified as a return of principal with no future taxation due.

We do not give tax advice, so please consult your CPA/Accountant on all areas of taxation and the tax treatment of all funds.

There are a number of riders, options, and alternatives available with annuity products. It is important to be aware of the options and how they can best be used to enhance and benefit your financial goals. There are also other benefits, which are normally included in an annuity contract for no additional cost. They are: full account value upon death, nursing home riders, and terminal illness riders. Even though you may still be in your surrender charge period, under these types of conditions, the surrender charge period is typically waived.

Long Term Care & Alternatives – I have touched on long term care in reference to accessibility to your annuity funds, but I have not addressed the issue of long term care insurance as part of your financial portfolio. There is no greater factor that can liquidate your estate faster than a long term illness. When an individual is placed into a nursing home or long term care facility, the first question the administrator will ask is: "How are you going to pay for it?" Even if you have the means to pay for it directly or personally, they still want to know about all your other assets in case you outlive your income and the State has to liquidate your assets to pay for your continued care to limit the State's future liability.

If you cannot afford long term care insurance, many individuals have found by withdrawing the interest only from their CD, savings, or annuity contract, it would be more than enough to cover the cost. If you do not qualify medically for long term care insurance, the greater the need becomes to have an annuity policy that offers living benefits, later in life.

There are living benefits in annuity contracts. Some benefits are automatic, some ask a few simple underwriting questions to qualify, and others that are available to you after a specified period of time (normally between 2 and 5 years).

That was a lot of information regarding annuities with riders, living benefits, options, and alternatives. I would even venture to say this is more information than you've ever thought you would ever hear about annuities. As you can see, having an annuity specialist can be an enormous benefit to you. Use their knowledge and expertise to determine the right annuity product that meets your specific needs and objectives to provide you with a financial benefit to last you a lifetime.

Variable and Fixed Indexed Annuities

I want to touch on the subject of variable and fixed indexed annuities. Both are great vehicles for any financial portfolio. I believe most professionals do not explain all the options and alternatives available to meet their clients' specific needs.

Variable Annuities – Variable annuity contracts are limited to the investment account or the sub-accounts, which are approved by the insurance company issuing the annuity contract. The number of sub-accounts offered may have limitations and/or differences compared to your own investment ideas within your financial portfolio. Variable annuity contracts also have surrender charges to help mitigate (not eliminate) the annual cost or fees associated with the variable contract. This is different from the asset fees, which are deducted from the account balances each year from the variable annuity contract.

You have full account value (either with gains or losses) based upon the performance of the investment accounts or sub-accounts. A variable annuity contract is subject to market volatility and does not offer minimum guarantees other than the possibility of a money market fund and/or a fixed account fund as one of the sub-accounts.

The number one complaint about variable annuity contracts is paying the asset management fee after experiencing major losses or declines in the stock market due to volatility. Variable annuity contracts can be a costly endeavor due to the fees associated with them in a decreasing market trend. Sometimes, having a crediting option that receives a zero return from a fixed indexed annuity can be a good thing, especially in years the market is down.

When you compare a variable annuity in years when the market is down, losses of -15% are going to cost you an additional -2% to -3% minimum, due to the M&E and asset management fees charged, for a total loss that can be as high as -18% to -20%. The market doesn't always move in a straight line up, rather it moves in peaks and valleys. *Will you be able to receive a greater rate of return than the fees paid out over the life of the variable annuity contract?*

If you have the income benefit rider, it will only compound the problem in variable contracts. The original deposit and the contractual 6% interest rate compounding annually for the income benefit rider are contractual guarantees, which must be reserved for the full income value by the insurance company. Any losses from the variable annuity sub-accounts would require additional reserves to cover the income benefit rider's full account value. This could result in the carrier increasing the cost of the rider (if possible) to offset the additional reserve requirements. The additional reserve requirements, due to previous losses, have resulted in many companies reducing or eliminating the income benefit rider, increased the cost of the rider's fee, and/or suspended the future sales of their variable annuity products and the income benefit rider.

Fixed Indexed Annuities - There are many things I do like about fixed indexed annuities. They do not have the fees typically associated with variable annuity contracts. They offer guarantees and the ability to lock-in the gain annually, based upon the annuity and crediting options chosen.

Using indices or indexes offers a broader diversification than sub-accounts in variable annuities, since indices may include over 500 or more companies and over 100 industry groups. Some of the indices date back to the 1920's and offer some of the biggest names in their industry. Due to the historic returns of some indices, they are used as a benchmark for investment managers to meet or exceed their expectations.

With fixed indexed annuities, you agree to receive a lower guaranteed rate of return in exchange to participate in the general account fund of the insurance company. Your funds are not invested directly in the market. The general account fund purchases large volumes of options at a discount. After the option has expired, the general account fund either made money or did not. If the general account made money, you participate in the gains. If the general account did not make money, your account is credited with zero, not the negative return of the market. You may not receive all the gains in an up market, but you do not share in any of the negative returns in the years when the market is down.

The cap rate, participation rate, and/or the yield spread control the cost of the options. They can be used individually, together, or as a combination of any and all of the above. No one knows what the future cost of the options will be. The cap rates, participation rates, and yield spreads are used to help control the future cost of the index options and give insurance companies alternatives on the options they purchase. Please review the options carefully in your annuity contract. It will provide all the disclosures on cost, options and fees associated with your specific fixed index annuity. I do not classify the yield spread as an asset management fee or asset fee because not all fixed indexed annuities have a yield spread. It is used as a tool to help insurance companies control the future cost of the index options only.

Fixed indexed annuities are a great safe money solution and a beneficial addition to any financial portfolio. If the market goes up, you're guaranteed to make money. If the market goes down, you're guaranteed not to lose any money. And if the market continues to go down constantly for the life of the contract, you are guaranteed not to lose your money since you have a guaranteed minimum interest rate declared within your annuity contract. The only thing you have to do is hold the contract to term, less any withdrawals or distributions received from the annuity.

If your objective is income, the income benefit rider will provide you with the highest guaranteed income stream in the industry, without annuitizing the contract GUARANTEED! Finally, should the market outperform the income benefit rider, your income stream is guaranteed to be enhanced by receiving the higher income payout, based upon the increase in your total account value.

Compensation – I wanted to disclose how the financial services industry is compensated. I know this is a subject that may be taboo to discuss, but I felt it is important for everyone to understand that absolutely no one in the financial services industry works for free. There are different levels of compensation and fees that are paid, but ultimately everyone does get paid. Sorry for bursting your bubble if you thought everyone is your friend. They're not, nor should you want them to be. They work with you for one purpose and one purpose only; to assist you with your financial portfolio. Yes, they are being paid whether you realize it or not, in the form of a commission by the insurance companies or an asset management fee by their Broker-Dealer. As I mentioned before, the relationship should be that of an employer/employee, when it comes to your financial portfolio.

Securities – Registered representatives are securities

licensed and are paid directly from their specific Broker-Dealer. They are normally compensated with a small commission, which is paid up front (between 2% & 4%), and the asset management fee, which is paid annually. The average asset management fee will vary between .15% to as much as 1.25% annually. Regardless of market performance, the registered representative will be paid a percentage of the asset management fee being charged.

Insurance Agents/Brokers – Insurance agents are paid a commission by the insurance company, not from the proceeds of the client. The commissions are paid up front based upon the life and/or the annuity policy being purchased, issued, and are directly linked to the surrender charge period. The commissions are higher for an insurance agent initially than for a licensed securities registered representative (normally between 2% to 8% on average for annuities and as much as 80% of the first year premium for the life insurance contract with a renewal of 1% to 3% annually). This is a one-time commission fee for annuities with no other commissions to be paid. There is no asset management fee. Again, the commissions paid out are directly related to the surrender charge of the life and annuity contracts.

A few insurance companies will offer a trail commission or asset trail commission, if the insurance agent/broker will accept a lower commission at the inception of the policy. The trail commission will normally begin in the second year and continue for as long as the policy is in force. This arrangement is similar to a securities licensed registered representative. The insurance agent/broker would initially receive between 2% to 4% of the first year premium as a commission and a trail commission that will range between .25% to as much as .40% annually beginning in the second year.

Banking Industry – The banking industry normally pays their tellers an hourly wage. When they reach the position of an account representative, customer service representative, or move through the ranks and qualify for a position as a bank manager or as an executive at the corporate level, they are normally paid an annual salary. The salary will vary based upon position and is usually capped at certain levels. Annuities are sold within each branch by the account representatives who are paid an additional $25 to $50 per annuity application or annuity product sold.

No Load Mutual Funds – You may be one of those individuals who believe everyone should work for free, so you only purchase no load mutual funds. I've got news for you: Even no load mutual funds can charge as much as 12% of the total asset value to market and promote their no load mutual fund in any given year.

It doesn't matter whether you are working with an investment advisor, financial planner, or an account representative; all are professionals in the financial services industry (providing you with recommendations, advice, products, and services), and should be compensated for the services they provide. Today, many companies provide full disclosure with respect to compensation paid to the advisors. Whether you believe they are being paid too much or too little should not affect the services they provide. Most commissions are pre-set and asset fees are predetermined (base upon the size of the investment account), so changing advisors will have very little impact at reducing the fees or commissions being paid. If you were receiving bad service and/or bad advice from your advisor, I would highly encourage you to make a change from your current advisor. In this particular situation, it is not the fee that is the problem, but the recommendations or advice from the advisor.

RULE 151A

Variable annuities are considered securities and are only sold through licensed securities representatives registered with FINRA (Financial Industry Regulatory Authority). Fixed indexed annuities are considered an insurance product and are only available through licensed insurance agents with no FINRA affiliation. Beginning on January 1, 2011, under Rule 151A, fixed indexed annuities will be classified as securities and will require all representatives to be securities licensed with FINRA to sell this product.

There is opposition to Ruling 151A by NAIC (National Association of Insurance Commissioners) and insurance companies who feel fixed indexed annuities should not be classified as securities since they offer full guarantees within the annuity contract.

As previously mentioned, the difference between insurance and securities is that insurance companies can use the term guarantees and securities firms can use the term investments. You will have to wait for the final outcome to see if fixed indexed annuities will be considered a securities product or not. Until then, they are still being sold as a non-securities product.

Fixed indexed annuities have many different crediting options available. They can range from an annual point-to-point, monthly average annually, monthly point-to-point, current crediting interest rates, or any number of combinations and alternatives listed above.

As previously mentioned in an earlier chapter, *"Rate of Return Comparisons"*, there are many different indices and they vary greatly based upon their specific crediting methods with the most common being the S&P 500 Index®. Today, you can choose between the DJIA®, Nasdaq 100®, and the S&P 500®. There are also global index strategies, which include the Nikkei 225®, EURO STOXX 50®, and the Hang Seng Index®, just to name a few.

For comparative purposes only, let's evaluate the performance of the S&P 500 Index®, a fixed indexed annuity using the S&P 500 Index® option crediting method, and the minimum guarantees of a fixed indexed annuity contract. The performance will be based upon a 10-year period beginning September, 1998 through September, 2008, with the initial deposit of $250,000.

The fixed indexed annuity used for this comparison was designed with an annual point-to-point option crediting method. It has the ability to lock-in positive gains each year the S&P 500 Index® option provides a positive rate of return. In the years the S&P 500 Index® option is down or in negative territory, the account value remains the same and the account is credited with zero, not the negative return reflected by the performance of the S&P 500 Index®.

This is to evaluate the power of being able to lock-in annual gains compared to the peaks and valleys of overall market performance. If the market performance has negative returns over the entire 10-year period, you are guaranteed to receive the minimum rate of return from your fixed indexed annuity contract.

September 1998 to September 2008

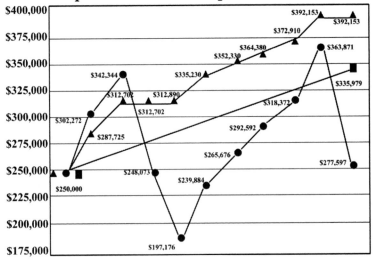

●Represents the S&P 500 Index® performance over a 10-year period, which does not have the ability to lock-in the annual gains.

▲Represents the S&P 500 Index® options using a fixed indexed annuity contract, which has the ability to lock-in the annual gains, with no negative crediting.

■Represents the minimum guarantees in the fixed indexed annuity contract.

This graph is based on actual crediting rates for the period shown; however, this is not an illustration and does not represent past or future performance. It is being used as a comparison between market performance using the S&P 500 Index® and S&P 500 Index® crediting methods using options. The purpose is to evaluate certain market conditions over a specified period of time only. This clearly demonstrates the limitations of fixed indexed annuities compared to the full growth potential of the S&P 500 Index® in years the market is up. It also reflects the potential of fixed indexed annuity crediting a zero rate of return in years the S&P 500 Index® is down or in negative territory, without having to participate or share in market losses.

This evaluation does not include any type of costs, fees, or dividend schedules associated with the S&P 500 Index® or the S&P 500 Index® Options. This is not to be interpreted as one strategy performing better than another, but rather how each account will perform differently under diverse market conditions. It provides an understanding of how market adjustments will affect market performance and the possible outcome of the results. With fixed indexed annuities, the account value does not receive the full value in the years when the S&P 500 Index® is up, but has the ability to lock in gains annually, without loss of principal, or being subjected to market risk.

Annuity Techniques

There are many techniques using annuities that can accomplish many different objectives. If you are looking to create an income stream and utilize the full tax benefits that annuities have to offer, no other technique accomplishes it more effectively than a split-annuity or annuity laddering as a concept and strategy.

Split Annuities – The split annuity income concept and strategy is nothing new and has been around for a long time. What makes it so beneficial is that it works well, especially if you understand the basic principal behind the concept.

The idea is to take your principal amount and split it between two annuities. Annuity #1 is used as an immediate annuity to generate the income over a 10-year period. Annuity #2 is the recovery annuity. This is the most critical part, since the recovery will be based upon the actual rate of return you will need in order to recover the original principal. The balance will be placed into Annuity #1 to fund the immediate annuity for income purposes. Annuity #2 uses the triple compounding effects of an annuity to recover 100% of the original principal. Here is an example of how the recovery works:

> **For Income Annuity #1: $44,000.00**
> **Annual Income Generated: $5,000.00**
> **Total Income Generated: $50,000.00**
>
> **Recovery Annuity #2: $56,000.00**
> **Rate of Return: 6%**
> **Recovery after 10 Years: $100,287.00**

Again, Annuity #1 is used as the immediate annuity to generate an income stream for the next 10 years.

Annuity #2 is designed to recover the original principal using the triple compounding effect. This is a way to use your funds to create an income without losing the original principal amount through the use of recovery.

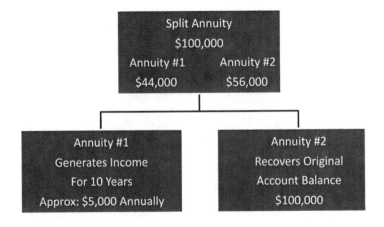

There are particular situations when an individual may need more income. By reducing the recovery amount to $50,000 we can increase the income over the 10-year timeline.

Annuity Laddering – Laddering is similar to a split annuity. However, instead of splitting a lump sum into two annuities, you are using three or even up to four annuities to create the income stream over a 15-year period with full recovery at the end of the 15th year.

Here is an example of how annuity laddering provides a complete income stream over the course of 15 years, on a tax-favored basis by using the exclusion ratios and providing full recovery. The client has $250,000 and would like to provide an income for his retirement. To make this easier to understand, I will explain the entire process in the order in which it will occur:

2009 – Initially set-up the $250,000 into four annuity products, with the first annuity as the immediate annuity to generate the first leg of the income stream and last annuity designed as the recovery ladder.

Annuity #1 – Deposit $70,230.88 into an immediate annuity, which will generate $14,593.08 of annual income per year for a total of 5 years.

Annuity #2 – Deposit $47,919.66 into a 5-year deferred annuity to earn a projected 5.50% rate of return annually.

Annuity #3 – Deposit $34,669.83 into a 10-year deferred annuity to earn a projected 6.00% rate of return annually.

Annuity #4 – Deposit $97,206.63 into a 15-year deferred annuity to earn a projected 6.50% rate of return annually to recovery the original account value.

2014 – At the end of the 5th year, annuity #1 (the first immediate annuity) has been completely paid out. At this point, we begin phase 2 with annuity #2 being transferred into an immediate annuity to begin the next income stream for the next 5 years, or until year 10 of the annuity laddering strategy.

Annuity #1 – Paid out a total of $72,965.40 over the 5 years of income. The account value is now zero with no future payment.

Annuity #2 – Account value is now $62,629.08 and will be placed into an immediate annuity to generate $14,666.25 of annual income per year for the next 5 years or until the 10th plan year.

Annuity #3 – The account value is now $46,396.05 and still growing for another 5-year period.

Annuity #4 – The account value is now $133,181.51 and still growing for full recovery in year 2024.

2019 – We are now at the end of the 10th year. Annuity #2 (the second immediate annuity) has been completely paid out. At this point, we begin phase 3 with annuity #3 being transferred into an immediate annuity to begin the next income stream for the next 5 years, or until the 15th year of the annuity laddering strategy.

Annuity #1 – Account balance zero.

Annuity #2 – Paid out a total of $73,331.25 over the last 5 years in income. The account value is now zero with no future payment.

Annuity #3 – Account value is now $62,088.39 and will be placed into an immediate annuity to generate $14,739.56 of annual income per year for the next 5 years or until the 15th plan year.

Annuity #4 – The account value is now $182,470.21 and still growing for full recovery in year 2024. This is also a good example of the power of the triple compounding effects using annuities.

2024 – We are now at the end of the 15th year.

Annuity #3 (the third immediate annuity) has been completely paid out. At this point, annuity #4 has completely recovered the original principal account balance of $250,000.00.

Annuity #1 – Account balance zero.

Annuity #2 – Account balance zero.

Annuity #3 – Paid out a total of $73,697.80 over the last 5 years in income or to the 15th year. The account value is now zero with no future payment.

Annuity #4 – The account value is now $250,000.00 and has been fully recovered in the year 2024. The individual used the funds available to generate an income without the risk of losing the original principal.

At this point, the individual has the choice to turn around and start all over again. If the need to increase the annual income is a priority, the annuity laddering strategy could be structured to reduce the recovery amount to a lower level and raise the projected income payout schedule.

The following is a graphic chart to illustrate the example used above on the annuity laddering concept and strategy.

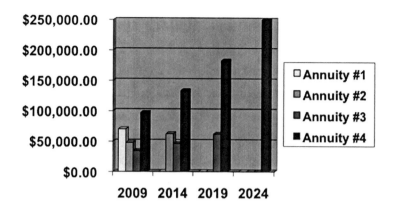

I would like to share a story with you. It's about the services we provide or should provide to our clients, as professionals in the financial services industry.

Last week, Joyce, a client I've had the pleasure of serving since the Spring of 2008, called to ask about a statement she received. It referenced an index strategy that was to be discontinued. Her statement had zeros across the page for that particular index strategy. I explained to her that this did not pertain to her, but was a notification to all annuity policy holders that the indexed strategy is no longer being offered as one of the index choices. She thanked me again for keeping her money safe and providing the income to allow her to live her life, after the loss of her husband.

Joyce's family, like so many families throughout America, relied on two incomes to make ends meet. She and her husband had built a good life together. In the Spring of 2008, her husband passed away suddenly from cancer. It was unexpected since he was in his mid 50's and Joyce in her mid 40's. He did everything right; he had one life insurance policy, which paid off the mortgage to the house; and a second life insurance policy, which provided $500,000 for Joyce and their two daughters.

After the funeral, she talked with her family and friends about what to do with her money. Some made suggestions about investing, while others recommended she speak with an investment advisor. She decided to make an appointment with several investment advisors to discuss her situation. They all had recommendations and different investment strategies and the income she could receive. There was one very big problem; they were not listening to her. You see, she didn't have a high paying job. She knew this was the most amount of money she would ever have and needed it to last her a lifetime. She could not afford to lose any money due to market losses. She needed to use the money to take care of herself and her two daughters.

She went to church and prayed about her finances and the concerns she had about the investment advisors she spoke with. A young woman approached Joyce to give condolences for the loss of her husband. They had seen each other in church over the years. Joyce asked the woman what she did for a living. She replied, "I am a financial planner". (Over the years, I have worked with many financial planners and she is one of them. Together, we design financial portfolios to meet the client's needs, objectives, and financial goals.) Joyce asked if she would be willing to sit down with her to go over her financial situation and she agreed.

After their initial meeting, they discussed Joyce's financial information in depth: her needs, her daughters, her concerns about the future, not having enough income to last her a lifetime, not wanting to lose any of her principal, and if she could, not having to work full-time.

The first thing was to establish an emergency fund, which was placed into a savings account. This was to provide her with the safety and security she so desperately needed; just in case something were to happen, she would always know that 100% of those funds would be available to her immediately.

Next, we established an income stream for years to come without liquidating her account balance and providing full recovery without the loss of principal. This is a technique that can only be guaranteed through the use of annuities. Again, this wasn't about anyone except Joyce and what she wanted to accomplish for herself and her family. This is a real person who needed very specific products to meet her financial needs.

In the last year, Joyce decided she could afford to work on a part-time basis, not because she needed to, but because she wanted to. Her oldest daughter just got married, and her youngest daughter began her first year in college. She still has her emergency fund that has more than $50,000 dollars in savings, and she receives her monthly check each and every month from the insurance company (which is automatically deposited into her checking account, so she can pay her monthly living expenses). She has not lost a dime due to market losses and is 100% debt free. She was able to accomplish all her financial goals using annuities, which provided the means of safety, security, and guarantees for her financial portfolio and her own peace of mind.

The annuity laddering strategy was implemented and put into action in June of 2008, just before the financial meltdown in September, 2008. We have all been affected in one way or another by the financial crisis of September, 2008. In this particular situation, Joyce knew exactly what she wanted and was not willing to accept anything less. What if Joyce didn't know what she wanted or could not express her specific needs properly to an investment advisor? What if she had listened to or had taken the advice from family and friends? What would have happened to her financial portfolio? Would she have been able to recover? How much would it have impacted her financial portfolio and her income? Would she have had to go back to work full-time? (Now you can understand why I do not recommend using family and friends for your financial portfolio or having your advisors as your friends.)

Through the use of the annuity laddering strategy and concept, we were able to meet all of her specific goals without placing her life savings at risk. If she were at a different point in her life, investing in the market may have been a great option, but not when considering her specific objectives and financial goals.

Additional Techniques for Income and Wealth Transfer Strategies

When we look at our current financial situation effecting the older population, they fall within two groups. The first group is struggling to make ends meet and living on a limited income. The second group has lost a percentage of their financial portfolio, but they have a good retirement income, which meets their needs and are using their investment account to leave a legacy to their children and grandchildren.

Even though they are both within the same age group, they have two completely different needs, each with a different solution. The first solution shows how to use your current assets to increase your monthly income; the second provides a means to re-coup against previous market losses and transfer a larger portion of your funds to your family members on a tax-free basis.

This is how they can work within the financial portfolio.

Reverse Mortgages – When reverse mortgages were first introduced in the mid 1990's, private investors funded the market in their entirety. Unfortunately, there happens to be many unscrupulous investors who used reverse mortgages as a ploy to acquire properties for pennies on the dollar and at the expense of many seniors. Unsuspecting seniors were charged high interest rates they could not afford and were forced into foreclosure by the same investors who promised to help them with their financial situation.

Since then, the reverse mortgage market is now 100% monitored and controlled by the U.S. Department of Housing and Urban Development (HUD). There are strict guidelines, which all banks must follow in order to participate in the reverse mortgage program, which does not include individual investors.

To qualify for a reverse mortgage, you must be at least 62 years of age. If you are married, the younger of the two must be at least 62 years old. To receive the maximum benefit from a reverse mortgage, an individual or couple must have little or no mortgage payments. In some situations, even though you may still have a mortgage payment, you may still qualify for the reverse mortgage. In place of receiving a monthly income or lump sum at closing, the savings is eliminating the monthly mortgage payment and keeping your money in your pocket, instead of continuing to pay your mortgage to the mortgage company.

For example, if your monthly mortgage payment is $1,200 dollars per month, by implementing a reverse mortgage you eliminate the monthly mortgage payment. This allows what you would normally pay for your mortgage payment to be added to your monthly disposable income. I recommend using annuities with living benefits to increase the income benefits in the future. The split annuity or the annuity laddering concept with full recovery would work well with the proceeds from the reverse mortgage program.

Before you can apply for a reverse mortgage, you are required to go through an education process that addresses the pros and cons of the reverse mortgage program. An approved HUD counselor must perform the counseling for the reverse mortgage program. Upon completion, you will receive a reverse mortgage certification that must be submitted with your initial reverse mortgage application before you can be considered for the reverse mortgage program. Once you have been approved, there are three requirements you are required to maintain with respect to your home:

- *Must reside within the home and be your primary residence*

- *Must maintain the house and property to an acceptable living standard*

- *Must keep current and pay all property taxes*

It's important to remember that should you need care in a hospital, long term care facility, or nursing home for a period beyond 6 months, you could forfeit all your rights for your house and the property to HUD. The same holds true if both the husband and wife should pass away. In both case scenarios, the family members have the right to purchase the house from the reverse mortgage lender. If not, HUD would sell the house and pay off the existing loan. If they're in the care of a hospital or nursing home facility, the funds will be used for their future care, and upon death, the balance would be placed into their estate for the benefit of their family members and heirs.

Over the years, I have seen many seniors with limited resources who refuse to evaluate the benefits of a reverse mortgage. In many situations, a reverse mortgage may be the only option to help offset their living expenses. Their thought is to leave the house to their children. They understand the benefits of a reverse mortgage and how it could improve the quality of their lives, but they choose to continue making sacrifices and struggling each month for the benefit of their children.

Whether you have a reverse mortgage or not, if you or your loved ones enter into a nursing home facility without the funds to pay for the care provided, the nursing home has the right to place a lien against the home for the future care of the patient.

Incidentally, did you ever ask your children if they wanted your house? In most cases, your children have their own homes with their own families, that best accommodates their own lifestyle. Most children would much rather have their parents as comfortable as possible in their golden years. They certainly do not want their parents to make sacrifices on their behalf.

In most cases, upon death, the house would be sold and the proceeds would be divided equally between all family members. If you have a choice of making sacrifices for your family or improving your own quality of life, please take care of yourself first! Enjoy the time you have – life is such a precious gift.

Single Premium Life Insurance – Believe it or not, transferring funds into a single premium life insurance policy is one of the best things you can do. If you are not going to use the funds and have already allocated the funds to your family members, life insurance is the most cost effective way to transfer funds tax-free. There are many advantages and benefits to using this strategy. Here are a few things to consider:

Face Value – If you are like millions of Americans who lost money in the market since September, 2008, you have a good chance of making up a large portion of those losses through life insurance. In most cases, you should be able to double your initial deposit for the face amount of the policy. For example, if you deposited $100,000 into a life insurance policy, in most cases, the face amount of the policy would be $200,000 or possibly higher. That is an immediate gain of 100% or an additional $100,000 to your family members.

Simple Underwriting – This policy is priced to allow for older age individuals who have standard medical conditions to qualify for life insurance. For older aged individuals, they can receive simple underwriting, meaning there is no medical exam, no blood withdrawal, and no urine specimen required. As long as your medical conditions fall within specific guidelines, the insurance company will issue the policy. The underwriting is for the net amount at risk. What that means is if you deposit $100,000 into a life insurance policy and the death benefit is $200,000 the underwriter will only underwrite for $100,000, since this is the total amount at risk to the insurance company.

Tax-Free – Life Insurance is the only vehicle that allows the proceeds to transfer 100% tax-free. Every other vehicle will be taxed to some degree, either as capital gains or as ordinary income. With the current state of the economy, we know taxes are going to go up. How much? No one knows. We do know it will have an impact on our economy for years to come. I can guarantee you one thing; the increase in taxes is going to be much higher than what we have experienced in our lifetime.

These are all great tools to be used to supplement your retirement income and to transfer assets on a tax-favored and/or tax-free basis. Most individuals like the idea of not losing control and not having to sacrifice principal to receive income. I'm sure there are a number of concepts and strategies that can easily meet your needs, in addition to the ones that have been described. Contact an annuity specialist to see what concepts and strategies will work best for your particular situation.

Hey…You Want to Know a Secret? It's called the Roth IRA…

Beginning in 2010, you no longer have the income restrictions and limitations to transfer qualified funds into the Roth IRA. The only thing you have to do is pay the taxes on the funds you convert to the Roth IRA. If you choose, you can transfer your funds over the course of 5 years, which will mitigate the tax liability over the same period.

Roth IRA - If you haven't thought about converting a portion or all of your tax-qualified funds into a Roth IRA, you should. This may be the last time you have the opportunity to capitalize on the transfer of tax-qualified funds into a tax-free retirement vehicle. If you are one of those individuals who have a tax-qualified retirement account, but were unable to convert to a Roth IRA due to your income limitations, now is your chance to capitalize on this tax advantage plan and convert your tax-qualified funds into a tax-free retirement income vehicle.

The only requirement is to pay the taxes on the transfer. All future gains are 100% tax-free and there is no requirement for minimum distribution at age 70½. Your funds can continue to grow without ever having to take a distribution.

This is an incredible opportunity for anyone who has a large qualified retirement account that can be transferred and converted to a Roth IRA to generate 100% tax-free retirement income.

When Should You Purchase an Annuity? TODAY!

We are living in a time of financial uncertainty. The financial crisis of 2008/2009 has impacted the price of homes and the rate of foreclosures in the housing industry. Unemployment has reached 10% and is expected to move higher. Virtually every retirement plan has suffered significant losses, to the extent many individuals feel they will never recover.

When you review the options and alternatives we have provided within this book, you will find that you have many choices, but you must act. No one expects our economy to recover for quite some time. I do expect a significant increase in inflation in the very near future. Annuities have different crediting options and alternatives that can benefit your financial portfolio and help you recover from market losses. What makes annuities different is the ability to change between fixed index crediting and current interest rates crediting annually. As interest rates increase, you can move your funds into the higher interest rate options to guarantee the current crediting interest rate each year, locking in the gains as your new account balance.

What will drive interest rates higher is our nation's inability to attract foreign investors. There will come a time when they will no longer continue to accept the risk at such a low rate of return, as our national debt continues to sky-rocket uncontrollably. Without providing higher interest rates for the risk involved, we will not be able to attract the investors needed to continue funding our national debt. Remember, in the last 12 months, we have added an additional $1.3 trillion to our national debt and the numbers keep growing.

The National Debt – According to the website "Truth in 2010", our current National Debt as of December 2, 2009 at 12:00 PM Eastern Standard Time was: $12,239,479,568,000.00 and growing...

Future Taxation – *"Based upon the information provided, do you think future tax rates are going to decrease or do you think they are going to increase?"* I've never had anyone tell me they thought the future tax rate was going to decrease, only increase!

It doesn't matter if you're a Republican, Democrat, Conservative, or a Liberal. Whether you supported Barack Obama or John McCain for President, this is an issue we will all have to face for years to come.

With the future increases in taxes and no one knowing the extent of the increases or how it will affect everyone financially, it is important to take full advantage of any products that can give you a tax advantage. What makes it so crucial is there is no telling when the tax laws may change and disallow the tax advantage products or make them no longer available. Typically, insurance products such as life and annuity products have been grandfathered under the old tax system and only affect new products and policies issued after a specified date.

Powers of Annuities – There are benefits associated with annuities that are only inherent to them. They offer guarantees, tax deferral, income exclusion ratios, and (in most situations) loan provisions for non-qualified funds as part of the annuity contract.

Safety, Security, and Guarantees – There is not another product available that offers the safety, security, and guarantees available from annuities. All annuities must reserve for any and all guarantees contractually. Even the guarantees offered through riders as part of the policy are contractually guaranteed. For example, the income benefit rider, which guarantees a income for life, or the living benefits allowing for future income increases, with respect to the inability to perform 2 of 6 activities of daily living (ADL), are contractually guaranteed.

Tax Deferral – It doesn't matter if your funds are tax-qualified or non-qualified, all funds within an annuity contract grow 100% tax deferred. This means you do not pay taxes on your money until you take a withdrawal or begin taking a distribution.

Exclusion Ratio – The exclusion ratio is unique only to non-qualified annuity funds only. When you liquidate an annuity policy to provide a lifetime income or income for a period certain, the annuity policy will spread the taxable portion over the life income or period certain to mitigate the tax liability.

Any other investment is based upon "Last In, First Out" (LIFO), which means when you begin to receive a distribution, all the money you receive is 100% taxable until you have withdrawn all your funds down to your original deposit or cost basis. Annuities allow you to receive both principal and interest that normally exclude the largest portion from taxation. The exclusion can reduce the taxable income and, in some cases, eliminate the taxation on your Social Security income. As you can see, there are many circumstances when an annuity can help you improve your particular financial situation.

I described how annuities are very versatile and can provide options and alternatives and have advantages and benefits that no other products or services can match. You can increase your income by using living benefits or activities of daily living (ADL) to your advantage. Finally, how you can diversify by using annuities to create a well-balanced financial portfolio that will give you safety, security, and guarantees.

The Biggest Mistakes You Can Make with Your Financial Portfolio

1. *Not taking full control or responsibility of your financial portfolio.* Do not let your investment advisor control your decisions when it comes to your investments. All investment decisions should be discussed in full detail, between you and your investment advisor. Do not let them brush over the details and make sure you understand all aspects of your financial portfolio.

2. *Purchasing annuities from your bank or P&C agency.* They typically have the worst rates available.

3. *Listening to and/or taking advice from family and friends.* If you take their advice and you lose a large percentage of your financial portfolio, will they replace the money you lost? Is it worth destroying the relationship?

Probably not!

4. *Thinking your investment advisor is your friend.* If they are, they shouldn't be. It should be more of an employer/employee relationship (since they do work for you) and held accountable for your financial portfolio's performance. You can't do that with friends.

5. *Defending your investment advisor after he/she has lost more than the industry average.* It's your choice, but I would think it's time to get a new advisor.

6. *Not seeking knowledge and advice from an annuity specialist.* This is the person who can help you the most.

7. *Not reviewing your financial portfolio on an annual basis.* If you're not reviewing your financial portfolio, who is? You're also giving the impression that you don't care if you make money or not. You need to hold the professional investment advisors accountable and the best way to do this is through annual reviews.

8. *Not ensuring that your financial portfolio is properly diversified.* Diversification includes CDs, annuities, stocks, bonds, mutual funds, etc. Investing in the stock market is only one piece of the puzzle and does not give you a

true picture of your entire financial portfolio!

9. *Not evaluating how each vehicle in your financial portfolio will be treated in reference to taxation purposes.* Will your investment account increase your income and require a percentage of your Social Security income to be taxed? Is the interest credited treated as income? Is it possible to reduce or eliminate taxation by deferring the interest earned? Currently, the capital gains rate for securities is 15%; this is all going to change. I would not be surprised to see the capital gains rate back to 28% from the Reagan Era, or possibly higher. There was a time when the maximum tax rate was as high as 91% in the 1960's. It may not seem like such a big deal yet, but one day it may be, especially if you're being taxed on 80% of your Social Security income.

10. *How can you protect yourself and your financial portfolio when 100% of your funds are subject to market risk?* **DIVERSIFY... DIVERSIFY... DIVERSIFY...!!!**

In Summary...

I believe in proper diversification and I do not believe you can accomplish this with 100% of your funds invested in the market. I am not opposed to investing in stocks, bonds, mutual funds, or CDs; I simply believe there are additional options and alternatives that are never talked about or discussed that should be considered as part of any financial portfolio. Using annuities as a part of your financial portfolio can be extremely beneficial. If not for any other reason, you are able to create a safe money solution above and beyond investing. As with any other element in your financial portfolio, annuities should be reviewed annually. Anyone who purchases an annuity and thinks it can run on autopilot is sadly mistaken and will never be able to maximize their return. Annuities provide safety, security, and guarantees. By completing an annual review, you have the opportunity to maximize your return simply by evaluating your crediting interest rates on a regular basis. Even if you have a 5-year multi-year guarantee product and the rate is guaranteed for 5 years, having an annual review will establish a procedure for your entire financial portfolio to follow. At some point in the future, the rates will change. If you request the annual review each year, your advisors will expect it and will continuously keep an eye on the performance of your financial portfolio. I strongly recommend meeting with your advisors annually to determine if each and every aspects of your financial portfolio still meet your objectives and your financial goals.

The future of taxation and the national debt is going to have a dramatic affect on everyone's financial portfolio for years to come, including yours. The advantage of annuities and the benefits they provide should be considered as an integral part of any financial portfolio. In order for you to be able to benefit financially, you need to act today. We do not know when the future tax laws will change, or how they will affect the tax deferral of annuities or other financial vehicles. There is one thing we do know; there are certainly going to be changes regarding the future tax code.

Annuities have been around for over two thousand years. When I think of annuities, I think of words such as: steady, consistent, conservative, growth, stability, longevity, endurance, fortitude, and strength. This would be similar to NASCAR racing. It's not always the fastest car that wins the race; it's the car that is steady and maintains a consistent speed. The driver who is steady and makes the least amount of mistakes is the one who wins the race.

I realize annuities may not be as sexy as stocks, bonds, and mutual funds. With annuities, there is no ticker going up or down that indicates whether your annuities had a good day, a bad day, or a great day. There are no symbols on the evening news showing where your annuities finished for the day.

What we do know is annuities won't lose money when the market is down. Annuities are steady. They get you home safe and secure. Anyone who's ever owned an annuity knows one thing: at the end of the day, they made money, regardless of how the stock market performed. When the night falls and long after the sun goes down, annuity owners can rest assured their money is safe!

Disclaimer

The Financial Insider's Annuity Guide was written to provide the average individual with information and a basic understanding of how annuities can benefit any financial portfolio. It contains generalized information and practices regarding the financial services industry and the roles of the advisors who service them.

It illustrates how an individual should properly diversify their financial portfolio. This consists of CDs, annuities, stocks, bonds, and mutual funds. All funds, regardless of how and where the funds are invested (both qualified and non-qualified funds), must be considered for proper diversification.

This book is not intended to promote one concept, strategy, or idea, but rather to provide the understanding that each individual has different needs that should be evaluated by a professional to find the best solution to meet their objectives and their financial goals.

Every attempt has been made to provide the

reader with the most current, accurate, and up-to-date information available. The information provided is considered to be truthful, honest, and accurate at the time this book was written. Many concepts and strategies described throughout this book may be subject to interpretation.

Insurance, investment, and banking institutions are structured differently from one another. This includes, but is not limited to, the products and services they provide and/or how their employees are compensated. They operate and provide various products and services for a fee. The fees may be derived in various ways, such as: basic flat fees, additional charges, costs, asset fees, commissions, etc. This information may be common practice; however, it is not necessarily considered to be the standard for each industry.

The Financial Insider's Annuity Guide was written in a simple, easy to understand format and does not include technical information or disclosures regarding the various concepts and strategies covered throughout this book. It is important to read all disclosures in their entirety. If you are uncertain about the wording or the interpretation of any and all financial contracts, consult your Attorney.

Occasionally, tax laws change which may affect the validity or the tax advantages of the programs described within this book. It is the responsibility of the reader to consult with his/her Attorney and Certified Public Accountant for the credibility and legality of these programs and how they may benefit him/her and their financial portfolio.

A well-balanced financial portfolio includes an investment account (stocks, bonds, and/or mutual funds), annuities, CDs, savings, checking, and an emergency fund that should be readily accessible at all times, in its entirety.

Each state typically offers a free-look provision to evaluate the insurance contract purchased and/or a rescinding period to make a binding contract null and void. Know your rights and verify with your State whether or not they require insurance companies to offer a free-look provision.

The Financial Insider's Annuity Guide does not sponsor, endorse, sell, or promote any insurance company, investments firms, banking institutions, or the products and services they provide.

Fixed indexed annuity products are not sponsored, endorsed, sold, or promoted by: Standard & Poors®, Nasdaq®, Dow Jones Companies®, Dow Jones EURO STOXX 50®, Nikkei 225®, Hang Seng Index®.

"Standard & Poors®", "S&P®", "S&P 500®", "Standard & Poor's 500®", and "500®" are trademarks of the McGraw-Hill Companies.

"The Nasdaq-100®", "Nasdaq-100 Index®", "Nasdaq®" and "OMX®" are registered trademarks of NASDAQ OMX Group, Inc.

"Dow Jones®", "Dow Jones Industrial Average®", Dow Jones Index®" are registered trademarks of the Dow Jones & Company. "Dow Jones EURO STOXX 50®" is the intellectual property (including registered trademark) of STOXX Limited, Zurich, Switzerland and/or Dow Jones & Company.

The Hang Seng Index® (the "Index") is published and compiled by Hang Seng Indexes Company Limited pursuant to a license from Hang Seng Data Services Limited. The mark and name Hang Seng Index® is proprietary to Hang Seng Data Services Limited.

The copyrights relating to the Nikkei Stock Average® ("NSA®") and intellectual property rights as to the indications for Nikkei, Inc. ("Nikkei®") and the NSA® and any other rights shall belong to Nikkei®.

Fixed Annuities and Fixed Indexed Annuities are products of the insurance industry and are not guaranteed by any bank or federally insured by the FDIC.

All insurance companies are contractually obligated to reserve for future liabilities. The policies issued are preserved and protected by the assets of the issuing insurance companies.

About the Author

James Matthew Edwards has served as a professional in the financial services industry for over 25 years. He has both directly and indirectly worked with over 10,000 clients through financial planners, insurance brokers, investment advisors, certified financial planners, CPAs, and attorneys. He has successfully transferred in excess of $100,000,000 to safe money solutions.

In 2007 and 2008, James hosted a radio show, "The Financial Insider", which aired every Sunday morning on stations WTNT and WRC in Maryland, the District of Columbia, and Virginia. He discussed many safe money solutions and how to protect your individual accounts by proper diversification for your entire financial portfolio. By properly diversifying, you're not subjecting 100% of your funds to market risk.

James does not believe in the approach that one size fits all. He believes each client should be evaluated independently to determine his or her specific financial objectives. The evaluation should also include the effects of taxation on their Social Security income.

James has served on several insurance companies' advisory boards for developing life and annuity products. He has also served on several technology boards to evaluate new technology and the impact it could have on the financial services industry.

He is the expert in helping individuals preserve, protect, and transfer their wealth. His goal is to improve each individual's standard of living and their quality of life.

Breinigsville, PA USA
22 January 2010
231192BV00003B/1/P